Remembering Mother, Finding Myself

A Journey of Love and Self-Acceptance

Patricia Commins

Health Communications, Inc.
Deerfield Beach, Florida

www.hci-online.com

Thank you to the following for permission to reprint the listed material:

"Intervals, Progressions," by Susan C. Waters. ©1985.

"Madonna and Child." ©1998 by Ingrid Sischy, first published in VANITY FAIR, reprinted with the permission of Liz Rosenberg and The Wylie Agency, Inc. No further use of this material shall be made without the express written consent of The Wylie Agency, Inc.

Jung, C. G.; ASPECTS OF THE FEMININE. ©1982 by C. G. Jung. Reprinted by permission of Princeton University Press.

From TALKING TO HEAVEN by James Van Praagh. ©1997 by James Van Praagh. Used by permission of Dutton, a division of Penguin Putnam, Inc.

From THE LIARS' CLUB by Mary Karr. ©1995 by Mary Karr. Used by permission of Viking Penguin, a division of Penguin Putnam Inc.

From THE FEMININE MYSTIQUE by Betty Friedan. ©1983 by Betty Friedan. Used by permission of W. W. Norton & Company, Inc.

From THE CLOUD OF UNKNOWING, James Walsh, ed. ©1981 by James Walsh. Used by permission of Paulist Press.

From SIMPLE ABUNDANCE by Sarah Ban Breathnach. ©1995 by Sarah Ban Breathnach. Used by permission of Warner Books, Inc.

Reprinted by permission of Louisiana State University Press from Alive Together: New and Selected Poems, by Lisel Mueller. ©1986, 1996 by Lisel Mueller.

Reprinted with the permission of Simon & Schuster from NO ORDINARY TIME by Doris Kearns Goodwin. ©1994 by Doris Kearns Goodwin.

Excerpts from Women Who Run with the Wolves by Clarissa Pinkola Estés, Ph.D., ©1992, 1995. All rights including but not limited to performance, derivative, adaptation, musical, audio and recording, illustrative, theatrical, film, pictoral, reprint and electronic are reserved. Reprinted by kind permission of the author, Dr. Estés and Ballantine Books, a division of Random House, Inc.

From Don't Block the Blessings by Patti LaBelle with Laura B. Randolph. ©1996 by Patti LaBelle. Used by permission of Putnam Berkley, a division of Penguin Putnam Inc.

Library of Congress Cataloging-in-Publication Data

Commins, Patricia
    Remembering mother, finding myself : a journey of love and self-acceptance / Patricia Commins.
      p. cm.
    ISBN 1-55874-666-8
    1. Mothers. 2. Motherhood. 3. Mothers and daughters. 4. Identity (Psychology).
    5. Interpersonal relations. I. Title.
HQ759.C7215   1999   99-12511
306.874'3—dc21   CIP

©1999 Patricia Commins

ISBN 1-55874-666-8

Publisher: Health Communications, Inc.
               3201 S.W. 15th Street
               Deerfield Beach, FL 33442-8190

Cover design by Andrea Perrine Brower

For Leona Long Crisafulli
1924 – 1986

And all mothers
everywhere

The photo that started it all: The search for this photograph prompted my journey to get to know my mother from a new perspective—woman to woman. Pictured here (left to right) are my aunts, Mary Helen Colloca and Jeanne Long Hamm; family friend, Jacqueline Jacobson; my mother, Leona Long Crisafulli, and family friend, Eris Colloca.

Intervals, Progressions

An order in the house
was the aim of your voice
as it passed through rooms.

Still, I once heard you alone,
singing. You were a new songbird
found its perfect voice, weaving
from note to note, key to key

e^1 to c^3, solo

dolce, dolente

soprano coloratura
and you still clipped your fingernails
wore no jewelry, for the harp
you played when very young.

Order in the house, the weaving
of my long glossy hair into braids
as I practiced piano.

The iron stomping across the board:
tomorrow's school dress, my father's shirt.
And you were tired at the sink

with dishes bought with coupons,
the milk and bread of respectability.

An order in the house.
It dug into your shoulders
the way the straps of dresses did,
as you grew into the bored shape
of housewives who lived near us.

Yet, when you thought you were dying
you slept each night under stars,
beneath the rubbing harmonious spheres.
In the hammock you fixed on Lyra
and knew from the stars' movement
the earth fell toward the next day's light.

You wanted to stay on earth.
It had to do with order.

–Susan C. Waters

Contents

Acknowledgments

$\mathcal{I}$ have been blessed by the love and support of so many people as I launched and completed this book. Among the many, many special people I wish to thank are my husband, Kevin, for his support and belief in me as a writer, and my son, Patrick, who has given me the gift of motherhood. My father, Patrick Crisafulli, for whom I am named, gave his support not only for this book but for every endeavor of my life. My sisters, Jeanine Crisafulli Zastawny and Bernadette Crisafulli; my brother-in-law, Ben Zastawny, and my niece, Stephanie Crisafulli, form the core of my extended family.

I wish to thank my aunts, the "other mothers" of my life, Jeanne Hamm, Jeanette Meylan, Rose Crisafulli, Margaret Crisafulli, Mary Helen Colloca, Geraldine Crisafulli, and Laraine Crisafulli, my godmother, Barbara Sabatini, as well as my many cousins, especially Colette Crisafulli Robinson, who always believed.

My dear friend and editor, Janie Gabbett-Lee, was the first to read this manuscript and the one who proofread it. I also thank JoAnn Haselbauer-Locy, Judy Jones Davila, Sandy

Karkowski, Susan Waters, Mary Lou Peter and all the women of Reuters; Betty Wemlinger, Marsha Meyer and Mary Favia; Linda Dillon, psychic and friend who never loses hope; and the phone, faxes and friendships at Borsellino Capital Management.

Special thanks to my agent, Ariela Briagh Wilcox, for her untiring support and belief in this book; my editor at Health Communications, Christine Belleris, who was the first to see the value and uniqueness of this work; and Allison Janse at Health Communications, who helped shepherd this book.

And most of all, I thank the women who shared their stories with me from the depths of their souls. Without you, this book would not have been possible.

Introduction

The Journey to Where We Began

*I*t began with a whiff of perfume, the lyrics to a song and a search for a photograph. These commonplace things triggered memories deep within myself that started me on a journey to get to know the woman who was my mother for twenty-six years and who, on a spiritual level, is with me still. My desire to understand her went beyond our relationship as mother and daughter. Indeed, I had to step outside the parent-child relationship to see her in a new light as the woman who came before me. From this perspective—minus all the emotional baggage and conflicts that so often burden the mother-daughter relationship—I gained a clearer view of the woman who gave birth to me and, through triumphs and failures, tried to get me ready for the world.

While mine has been a solitary journey, I am not the only traveler on the path. I have spoken with more than one hundred women about their mothers, as well as experts from psychics to psychologists, counselors to clergy. I talked with women ranging in age from their mid-twenties to their eighties. What I came to understand in my own life, I found reflected in the lives of these other women: Until we understand our mothers as women, we cannot truly appreciate and accept ourselves.

Issues with our mothers do not end with their deaths. Throughout our lives we continue to seek their praise, find their favor, work to please them. And, to be honest, we still hear their critical voices ringing in our ears when we fail to live up to our own expectations. Whatever the emotional state of our relationships with our mothers—warm and nurturing or cold and distant—it echoes in our lives. Whether we miss our mothers' companionship or harbor unresolved anger and resentment toward them, these key issues will resurface throughout our lives.

Sometimes these issues seem to sneak up on us, triggered by life-cycle events—a marriage or the birth of a child, a divorce or serious illness or the death of a loved one. We miss our mothers when we celebrate, wishing they could share our joy. We feel abandoned by them when they are not here to comfort us in our distress. Our mothers are madonnas one moment and bitch-queens the next. We love them; we hate them.

Then I found a way to understand my mother and, in the process, to accept myself. I call it the Path of Understanding, a lifelong journey to remember, heal, continue and nurture our relationships with our deceased mothers. We find ways to resolve the mother-daughter issues and conflicts that remain. By delving into memories and seeking a connection through our own lives, we can experience a positive, ongoing relationship with our deceased mothers. Through meditation or simple life rituals, such as cooking from family recipes or wearing a piece of our mothers' jewelry, we daughters can bring the spirit, or essence, of our mothers into our present-day lives.

We are released from the sorrow that entraps so many of us daughters whose mothers have died.

The focus of this book is not on our mothers' deaths, but rather on the opportunity to get to know them in a new way—as the women who came before us. We learn to nurture the positive relationship that can exist between mother and daughter when we accept them for the women they were, as human beings with all the faults and frailties that come with the territory. We do not turn our mothers into saints, nor our lives into living monuments to them. Rather, we take an honest look at our mothers as a means to understand them and connect with them once again. That is the journey of this book. The destination is a fuller acceptance and love of ourselves. As Martha Borst, president of Phoenix 2000, lecturer on self-discovery, explains, "Until we are complete with our parents, we cannot be complete with ourselves."

Ideally, seeing our mothers as women is something we should do while they are still alive. In fact, while the focus of this book is for women whose mothers have died, the lessons and exercises are applicable to all mother-daughter relationships. Daughters whose mothers are still alive can benefit from the same perspective shift.

"It should be part of a woman maturing," suggests Nancy Friday, author of the breakthrough book on mother-daughter relationships, *My Mother, My Self*. "A woman needs to understand what she loves about her mother, and what she didn't like so much. That process should begin as soon as you think of yourself as an adult woman."

The truth of the matter, Ms. Friday explains, is that there are parts of our mothers—and all people with whom we have a relationship—that we don't like. When it comes to our mothers, we can still love them and be grateful for the nurturing we did receive from them, and yet acknowledge that we didn't like—or even hated—their attitudes about men and sex, their critical voices, how controlling we perceived them to be, or whatever.

The danger, Ms. Friday adds, is that if daughters don't take that honest look at their mothers before they die, we make our mothers into monuments. "We make her into a saint. We do that by being just like her—the good and the bad," she explains. But seeing our mothers as they were, separating the positive from the negative, we can honor and emulate the nurturing aspects we experienced, while rejecting the damaging ones. That, she adds, is the way to build a "good monument to her."

For those of us whose mothers have died, it is not too late to get to know them again. In fact, this process is crucial. It is the only way to understand this relationship that continues in our lives, long after our mothers' deaths; to unlock the negative patterns that repeat in our lives, in our other love relationships and, God help us, in our relationships with our own children. And for those who have enjoyed a full relationship with their mothers and grew to see them as women, it is a way to keep them in our lives in a healthy and nurturing way.

The key, once again, is the Path of Understanding. It is the "Aha!" we exclaim when we finally unlock this glorious puzzle that is our mother and find the missing piece that makes ourselves complete. We stop being children and look at our mothers—and ourselves—as adults.

"You don't need her in that two-year-old way," Ms. Friday says. The two-year-old who is so dependent, so demanding that her mother pick her up, feed her, play with her, acknowledge her, doesn't exist anymore. She has grown into a woman with the capacity to understand herself and her mother, both with their limitations. "My mother didn't have the capacity to pick up little two-year-olds," Ms. Friday continues. "But she was full of fun. . . . She had joy and creativity, and I've got that. She did what she could do. . . . She did her best with what she had. She wasn't perfect."

She wasn't perfect. For daughters looking at their mothers, there is no more powerful statement. When we allow our mothers to have been human, we stop demanding that they be perfect. When we accept the fact that the one with whom we had the first relationship in our lives was not always capable of meeting all our needs, we free her and ourselves. Then the truly miraculous happens. We stop demanding this same masochistic perfection of ourselves. We stop believing that we won't be loved unless we're perfect. We can't be perfect any more than our mothers were. We can try to improve, we can develop ourselves, we can be more aware, we can seek to become more spiritually enlightened. But we never will reach perfection; not on this planet. We will love the best we can.

This is the self-acceptance we gain from walking the Path of Understanding, when we choose to be governed no longer by the thoughts, fears and insecurities that stem from our childhoods. We step out in strength and in understanding, guided, I believe, by the love we experienced from our mothers and from the "other mothers" of our lives. As adult daughters, we look to the women who came before us and ask, "Who are you really? What were your hopes and dreams? What were your fears and insecurities? How is my life different from yours today? What do you have to teach me?"

On the Path of Understanding, we daughters seek to learn more about our mothers as individuals, in the context of the events, circumstances, and social and cultural influences in their lives. More fully understanding these factors, we see why our mothers believed and behaved as they did and, by extension, how these attitudes and actions affected our lives. This book uses stories, advice and exercises to help us see a fuller portrait of our deceased mothers as women. We grasp a deeper understanding of how our families functioned and why certain patterns, positive and negative, repeat in our lives. We see how we are remarkably like our mothers and how we are decidedly and rebelliously different.

But most important, we see the women who were, and on many levels still are, our mothers.

The Journey Begins

My mother died in June 1986, when I was twenty-six years old. She was diagnosed with colon cancer in February of that year, and within four months she was dead. We had just enough time to say good-bye, but far too few days to come to any understanding of each other and our sometimes conflicted relationship. I still remember her last words to me, as I left for the airport to fly from northern New York State, where I grew up, to New York City, where I was living then. She told me that she loved me. My mother was not demonstrative and she guarded her emotions. All these years later, I still feel the tug in my chest and the tightness in my throat as I hear in my mind those three words: "I love you. . . ."

When I started this book, my mother had been dead for a third of my life. At first, the idea of re-examining my relationship with my mother was a scary one. Who knew what dark secrets and negative emotions lurked in the corners of my psyche! Besides, I was over the grief, beyond the pain and in control of my life. I was at peace with myself and with her memory. I didn't have any unfinished business with her or issues to discuss. And in case nobody noticed, the woman was dead and therefore incapable of having any kind of relationship with me.

Or so I thought.

The truth was, I had dragged around old mother-daughter baggage for more than a decade, from relationship to relationship, job to job, and even into my own role as a wife and mother. I did have unfinished business with my mother, issues that only she and I could deal with. Those issues often took the form of beating myself up for mistakes I made, for things I didn't try and things I did. I had a hard time accepting the notion of being loved, and nothing I did or accomplished ever seemed to be good enough. I had created a monster mommy who criticized every step I took off the beaten path of my life. I assumed my mother would not approve of me simply because I was not comfortable with my own life and the choices I had made.

The Motherless Martyr

After my mother's death, I kept plowing forward in my life, trying to stay ahead of the pain. I endured a broken engagement and ended another relationship after that. I no longer experienced the positive nurturing of a mother in my life because I had banished myself to a motherless martyrdom.

Then, six years after my mother's death, I married my husband, Kevin, and six months later was happy to discover I was pregnant with our son, Patrick. I was so wrapped up in the excitement that I did not consider what it would be like for me to have a child without my mother.

This is a common occurrence for many women, even years after their mothers have died. Long after the grieving is over, life events can revive unresolved issues between a mother and a daughter. In my case, since my mother was dead, I did not reach out for any mothering when my son was born. In fact, I turned down offers of help. My attitude, while I may not have verbalized it at the time, was, my mother is dead. I have to do without.

Finally, exhausted from too little sleep, I admitted the truth to myself: I missed my mother. If she had been there, our apartment would have been cleaned, our meals would have been cooked and I would have been able to rest during the day. She would have done so much, I probably would have resented the hell out of her.

Realizing how much I missed my mother did not make me fall apart. Rather, it opened up a deep longing to get to know my mother again. Over the course of the next few years memories I had long suppressed began to resurface. One day while jogging—something I do, like my mother did, to keep slim—I smelled Shalimar, the perfume she often wore. I stopped in the middle of the block and looked around; there was no one in sight. I tried to shrug it off, but the memories that scent evoked were too powerful to ignore. I recalled my mother, in a suit, matching hat and high heels, sitting like the Duchess of Windsor in the back of my fifth grade classroom on parents' day. I slouched at my desk, torn between being proud of how beautiful she looked and being mortified at how different she was from everybody else's parents.

The smallest things began to trigger more recollections. One day while out for another jog, I heard one of my mother's favorite songs blasting from my headset. The music took me back to a summer day when I was a child in my bedroom, and a warm breeze billowed out the butterfly-printed Priscilla curtains on the window that looked out to the backyard. There, in a pair of baggy jeans and one of my father's old shirts, was my mother at the clothesline, singing "Good Morning, Star Shine" at the top of her lungs.

She never got the lyrics right.

The Invitation

During Christmas of 1996, I felt the most powerful tug of all. We spent the holiday with my family in my hometown of Oswego, New York. The three sisters—Bernadette, Jeannie and I—laughed and talked more easily with each other than ever before. On Christmas Eve, Kevin, Patrick and I squeezed together on a bed and a futon in the room that had been mine growing up. I tossed and turned, just as I had when I was a youngster so eager for Christmas that I could not sleep. But it was not the prospect of presents that kept me awake. Finally, in the wee hours of Christmas morning, I got up. I sat alone on the living room floor, sorting through a box of photographs. I sifted through loose snapshots that spanned forty or fifty years, in no particular order.

Like an archaeologist pawing through shards of rock, I kept digging, looking for a particular snapshot that I remembered but had not seen in years. Halfway through the carton, I feared the photo had been lost. Then I found it. The photograph had been taken at a New Year's Eve party in December 1961. In it, Mother, wearing a strapless gold brocade cocktail dress, poses with her sister, sister-in-law and two family friends. They were all beautiful, but my eyes return to my mother, who playfully hikes her skirt up to her knee. She was about thirty-seven in this picture—the same age I was when I began this book—and scandalously gorgeous.

A copy of that photo is beside me as I write this. Why, I ask myself, after all these years did I feel such an urgent need to possess this picture? On one level I realized that I was coming to terms with my own femininity and what it means to be an attractive woman, confident with herself. The need to understand and love myself sent me back to my beginning—to the woman I loved, admired, fought with, emulated, competed against, and then lost too soon.

But the photograph held something more. It was an invitation to get to know that woman in the gold dress, to understand who she was, the problems she faced, the dreams she realized and those she did not or could not. My desire to get to know my mother spawned this book, which serves as a road map for daughters seeking greater understanding of themselves and the women who came before them.

An Ongoing Relationship

If you think it is impossible to have a relationship with someone who is deceased, you're wrong. I'm not talking about a psychic connection (although I do not rule that out). What many women experience is an internal relationship with their mothers, intertwined with their own self-esteem and the way they view others. We contain within ourselves our perceptions of how our mothers felt about us. We feel their approval and their disapproval, regardless of the fact that death has ended the day-to-day activities we shared with them. Just think of the times you've said to yourself, "If Mom were here, she'd be so proud right now." Or, "If Mom were alive, she'd be having a fit."

We carry our mothers inside of us psychically just as they

once carried us physically. But now we have a chance to delve into those memories and feelings, to sort out the truth from the perception. We give ourselves permission to be honest with ourselves and our mothers, to express feelings long suppressed. We seek a broader and more complete portrait of these women by talking with others, filling in the gaps in our own memories and experiences. We look beyond the mother to find the woman.

In cases where a daughter had a traumatic, damaging relationship with her mother, healing is still possible. It begins with an honest acknowledgment of the pain endured in this relationship in which a mother, because of her own illness, addictions or other problems, was unable to love and care for her child. Pain acknowledged can be healed, allowing a woman to draw into her life nurturing from other sources, including herself.

We need to put our mothers' lives in context, culturally, historically and generationally. Knowing that a 1950s woman faced few choices in her life beyond her home and husband went a long way to explaining my mother's near-obsession with housework. Understanding that her generation, having survived the Depression and World War II, had become experts in "keeping a stiff upper lip" and "doing the best you can with what you've got" helped me realize why she wasn't driven to expect more in her life. The vast differences I saw when looking at her life and mine were no longer unfathomable chasms.

All of us, to some extent, wrestle with our relationships with our parents. It is, quite simply, part of growing up. But for women whose mothers have died, there is a special need to understand this relationship. We need to bring our relationships with our deceased mothers into the present moment—

regardless of what it was like when they were alive. When my mother died, for example, I was searching for my own way in the world and challenging everything I thought my mother stood for, from taboos against premarital sex to limited choices for women's lives. But later, as a wife and working mother in my thirties, I needed to bring my relationship with my mother into the present framework of my life. I no longer needed to rebel against her. I wanted to get to know her, woman to woman, to understand her life as I examined my own. I did not have a perfect relationship with my mother; such a thing does not exist. Ours was a typical, conflicted mother-daughter relationship. Our similar intense personalities and hair-trigger tempers made for some interesting "discussions" over the years. In my early twenties I tried to be as different from her as I could. But after her death, as I settled into my thirties, marriage and motherhood encouraged me to see what I could gain from my mother. I found that we are not all that dissimilar at the core.

More important, I have come to know the woman who was my mother—the funny, beautiful, caring, supportive individual who could also be a little distant and critical at times. She is not just a parent to me anymore, nor a memory or an old photograph. She is a presence in my life, psychological and spiritual. That is what I learned and gained on the Path of Understanding, which I lay out in this book.

Out of Sight, But with Us Still

Other women have been fortunate enough to have worked out many of their issues and conflicts while their mothers were still alive. As adult women, they reached a point of friendship with their mothers. What they often experience after their mothers' death is a loss of that closeness. They may be philosophical about it, telling themselves they were lucky that Mom lived as long as she did. But what many women do not fully realize is that their mothers are with them still. While the day-to-day activities are different—we cannot chat anymore on the telephone—the love remains.

Reverend Janet Campbell, canon of St. James Episcopal Church in Chicago, shares this example for understanding how death need not separate us. As tiny infants, she explains, we perceived that everything that was out of our sight was gone forever. Think of the child who drops a ball and, unable to go after it, thinks it has disappeared. Child psychologists tell us that very small infants literally forget we exist when we walk out of the room. They cry and we reappear, and they forget we were ever gone.

But there comes a point in children's development when they know that the ball has just rolled around the corner. They reach out for it, knowing that it will be restored to them. In the same way, we daughters can no longer see or touch our mothers. They have gone "around the corner" and out of our sight. But we know they are still there, and many of us believe that one day they will be restored to us.

The Motherhood Lesson

"I understood my mother better after I became a mother." In the interviews I conducted as part of my research for this book, I heard this statement dozens of times. It's a truism that I discovered in my own life. The reason, I think, is that we often experience exactly what our mothers did—both the joys and the frustrations. When the baby spits up on a silk blouse that has been out of a dry cleaner bag for less than ten minutes, it

reminds us of the time when we, as children, smeared choco-
late pudding on the dining room wall fifteen minutes before
company showed up.

But it's beyond empathy. As we raise our own children—or
become involved in the lives of nieces and nephews, stepchildren and friends' children—we literally relive issues from our
own childhoods. We understand firsthand the anxiousness our
mothers felt each time we headed out the door, and why we
received a litany of warnings instead of encouraging words.
And we come face to face with some of the void we felt when
our mothers were not "there" for us. We overcompensate with
our own children trying to satisfy the child inside us.

As I mentioned earlier, my mother was not particularly
demonstrative in her affection. I, on the other hand, dole out
hugs and kisses quite easily. But that difference between us
does not mean that I love my son more than my mother loved
me. Rather, I have come to understand that my love of my
child stems in part from my mother's love of me. What is different, however, is our expression of that love. My mother
loved in her service to her home and her family. Love was
expressed in an immaculately clean house, home-cooked
meals and fresh-baked bread. I took these things for granted
when I was growing up. But now I see the enormity of what
she did. She gave us comfort, security and nurturing each time
she clipped the laundry to the clothesline and kneaded the
dough on the bread board. In my life at the moment, I do not
have the time or ability to do those same things for my family.
And if I am truthful, I do not have the desire, either. But I can
celebrate the differences in my life compared with my
mother's, as much as the similarities.

Since I began this project, I have talked with more than one hundred women about their mothers. Their stories are reflected in this book. I am grateful for the honesty of these women as they talked about their mothers. Some of the women I had known before; others were strangers whom I heard about from other sources, or whom I met via the Internet. By the end of the conversation, I had forged a bond with another daughter who was dealing with an ongoing relationship after her mother's death. I must say, without exaggeration, that I received unconditional love and support from these women as I wrote this book. Their enthusiasm and strength helped carry me forward. Their belief in the need for this book helped make it a reality.

This book follows a sequential outline, beginning with the Call to Connection, which examines the need to get to know one's deceased mother. We are drawn to old photographs, particularly ones taken when our mothers were young women, before they married or when we were only babies in their arms. My mother was thirty-five when I was born, just a couple years younger than I am now. What was she like then, I wonder. If she were the woman next door, would we be friends?

The book then moves to examining the feelings that remain after our mothers die. These feelings become key signposts toward healing as a daughter follows the Path of Understanding. Too often we suppress these feelings, afraid and ashamed of our feelings of guilt, anger and resentment. Or we miss our mothers so much, we try to avoid the feelings of sadness and mourning in hopes of anesthetizing ourselves. But those feelings are never far from us, and very often are the same emotions that surface in other areas of our lives.

We begin to get to know our mothers the way a journalist investigates a story. We talk to people who knew her—but from a perspective that is different from ours. We talk with her peers, her family members and our own friends who remember her. Talking with our mothers' peers not only provides information about them, it forges a connection with a generation of women who came before us. We see through their eyes what our mothers were like as young women and why their friends liked them.

By talking to our own friends who knew our mothers, we gain a unique perspective. Our friends experienced our mothers during the same time frame as we did, but they have an entirely different reference point: they saw our mothers as women, while we experienced them as parents. JoAnn, who has been my friend since we were thirteen years old, saw my mother as a charming, lively woman who always turned an upbeat face toward the world. Through JoAnn I also saw the woman who could be kind, supportive and compassionate. JoAnn recalled the pep talk my mother gave her as she was trying to lose weight after her second child was born.

This book also helps us deal with painful memories and traumatic experiences. While we do not excuse any negative behavior or attitude inflicted upon us, we try to understand the cause. Very often our mothers lashed out at us because of pain, trauma or abuse in their own lives. Understanding these causes, we can separate ourselves from the pain of the past and begin to heal at our cores.

Understanding our mothers as women, we look at the times and circumstances they grew up and matured in. We look at the archetypes of their eras from the 1920s to the 1960s, from

Flapper and Social Worker to Rosie the Riveter, Donna Reed and Flower Child. "I am both a historian and the daughter of a woman who lived an interesting life, in that she grew up in the flapper era, was a social worker in the thirties (receiving an advanced degree in social work from Radcliffe), then married and raised five children in the forties and fifties," explains Cynthia, a student of history in her forties.

As we get to know our mothers again, they never cease to surprise us. Connie, a historian in her fifties, recalls being at a symposium held by the Ukranian leftist community a few years ago in Canada. While there, she was looking at some old photographs on display. "As I looked over a formal group photo of some women dressed in early forties style, I exclaimed, 'Oh God, it's my mother!' My husband took glee in proclaiming, 'Baba was a Commie!' Purely in jest, of course," Connie says. But she began to wonder just how left-leaning was her mother, whom Connie's children called "Baba," Ukranian for grandmother.

We also honor the other mothers of our lives, the women who raised us when our biological mothers could not, or those who gave us supplemental care and nurturing. The presence of these women in our lives is crucial, particularly if we had difficult or traumatic relationships with our own mothers. Knowing that other women cared and mothered us, we can draw that nurturing into our lives again.

Many women experience their deceased mothers as a kind of angelic presence in their lives, watching over them and their families. These women describe dreams and experiences that speak of love that continues beyond the grave. Their stories are inspiring and hopeful for the rest of us, whether we see our connections to our mothers in a psychological or spiritual light.

We examine the ways we honor our mothers, from everyday activities to special tributes. We are our mothers' legacies as their hopes and dreams are fulfilled in us. We become the doctors and scientists they did not; we create the art and music they could not. To honor their lives, as well as our own, we may be moved to acknowledge formally our mothers with scholarships, charitable work or even a Web page.

Finally, we celebrate ourselves. With the knowledge of our mothers and our beginnings, we move to the center stage to explore our own lives. As women today, we are juggling and defining many roles, from corporate executive to soccer mom. As we examine our lives, we define the legacy we will leave to those who follow us.

This book is experiential. Each chapter closes with suggested exercises to help women on the Path of Understanding. For that reason, readers may want to have a notebook and pen at hand. These exercises include the meditative Mother Walk, in which we envision our mothers in our lives today, a letter-writing ceremony to commit our deepest feelings to paper, and investigative tasks such as researching the eras in which our mothers were born and raised. Although this book has a spiritual overtone due to the nature of the subject, it is nondenominational and reflects stories of women from a variety of cultures, religions and backgrounds.

Our Mothers as Teachers

Our mothers were the first teachers we had. They introduced us to solid food, helped us take our first steps and taught us to blow our noses. Their views of the world became ours in those early days. Later we made our own choices, accepting some of our mothers' views and probably rejecting a lot more. As we get older, there is likely a point at which we realize that we've become a lot more like our mothers than we thought possible. Or we may choose to live an alternative lifestyle that is the polar opposite of the life our mother led.

Beneath the surface of our lives, our mothers still have lessons for us to learn. In some cases, it is a lesson in coping or compromise. In others, we learn not to make the same choices they did. In either case, we identify the issues our mothers dealt with as women, whether they went through the worst of the Depression or the heady freedom of the sixties. We look at our mothers without judgment to discover the essence of who they were as individuals.

Women I talked to have described their mothers as being "typical" of their eras, women who made do in hard times, who didn't contradict their husbands, and who endured lonely or disastrous marriages because of financial insecurity. Others speak of their mothers as being ahead of their times, pursuing—or wanting to pursue—dreams of higher education and developing inborn talents. A lot of would-be opera singers sang in the church choir. Many would-be surgeons attended scraped knees at the bathroom sink. We learn from them and their lives as we come to understand and accept our own. As we become more comfortable with our mothers and our beginnings, we stop being so hard on ourselves. Self-acceptance replaces self-loathing. We discover that we are, indeed, flawed. Then we join the human race with empathy and compassion. We can still have lofty goals and personal standards, but we no longer use those aims to chastise and punish ourselves. We love ourselves into wholeness.

The Gift of Our Families

There is a school of thought that, as souls before our birth into humanity, we choose our families. In her bestselling book *Embraced by the Light,* in which she chronicles a near-death experience, author Betty Eadie eloquently describes souls choosing not only their families but their life conditions. To some this may be poetry, to others it may be preposterous. But it offers an interesting perspective either way.

We cannot change the families into which we were born, whether we had a traditional nuclear family with two parents and siblings, or were raised by others. But what if we decided to look for the particular life lessons in those circumstances instead of just complaining about how things were? That's not to play the Pollyanna, saying everything was wonderful when it was not. But what if the good, the bad and the ugly of it all somehow made a deeper sense from the perspective of generational knowledge?

What if we daughters had the unique opportunity to understand fully the lives of the women who came before us? What if that knowledge and perspective helped empower us to make better choices for our own lives? What if the perspective of standing shoulder to shoulder with our mothers, as equals, helped heal the pain we experienced as daughters?

It would mean freedom and healing. The negative thoughts and behaviors that stretch, unconsciously perhaps, from generation to generation would be broken. We would no longer add our link to that chain of negativity. Our legacy to the next generation would be one of empowerment, hope and self-love. It would change the world.

A Grander View

Perhaps that sounds a little grandiose, being able to change the world simply by coming to understand our mothers. But what is the root of so much of our behavior, both the positive and negative? Aren't we all acting out old patterns, seeking to satisfy appetites for love, warmth and nurturing that stretch back to the cradle? How many of our love relationships are scarred by old hurts that go back to our parents?

The only way to break those negative ties is to understand them. The only way to find the love we lack is to go back to the beginning. The only way to understand where we are now is to look at where we began. The only way to appreciate ourselves as women is to understand our mothers from the same perspective.

Those are the lessons our mothers have for us. All we have to do is look inside ourselves to begin.

On this journey it is essential we remain true to ourselves and our feelings. We cannot rush the process by declaring, "My mother was a wonderful woman and I'm lucky she was in my life" before we truly get to know her. That's a little like falling in love with someone before the first date. Yes, those feelings may be there, but they won't be grounded, and the first conflict could shatter a delicate relationship. If you have anger toward your mother, acknowledge it. If you miss her so much you feel sick inside, acknowledge it. If you are so conflicted you don't know how to feel, acknowledge that, too. It's all honest, and there is no right or wrong to those feelings. I spent too much time in my life thinking I had to be perfectly at peace with my mother and then deciding I had to hate her, when I simply had to be.

So here is our mission statement as we begin this journey:

**I seek to understand my mother as a woman,
to learn the lessons from her life in
order to love and accept myself.**

Remembering Mother, Finding Myself is a journey that has already begun. We have all the resources we need to more fully understand our mothers and ourselves. All we need to continue is the desire.

The Call to Connection

> *"This is the mother-love, which*
> *is one of the most moving and unforgettable*
> *memories of our lives, the mysterious root of all*
> *growth and change; the love that means homecoming,*
> *shelter, and the long silence from which everything*
> *begins and in which everything ends."*
>
> —C. G. JUNG, *ASPECTS OF THE FEMININE*

eath does not end a relationship. Spiritually or psychologically, a thread remains, stretching from this world to the next. Through this connection, we feel the pull to understand our deceased mothers, to put into context not only their lives but ours. This understanding also answers the persistent question of "why" that nags us, threatens our self-esteem, sabotages our plans and taints our relationships. Why did she treat me like this? Why did she endure that relationship? Why didn't she pursue her dream? Why didn't she love me the way I needed to be loved? Why?

The answers are within us and around us, and the spirits of our mothers are willing to share them.

The Call to Connection can come at any time after a mother's death. For some it is an extension of the grieving process, a desire to keep a mother's memory alive. For others, including myself, it is a desire that surfaces many years later to understand who our mothers were. Regardless, it is at the heart of the Path of Understanding, the start of a journey to deeper understanding and profound healing. It begins with an acknowledgment that our mothers, regardless of how "good" or "bad" we judge our upbringing to have been, were an indelible force in the shaping of our lives.

Mother Denial

After our mothers die, there is a tendency by some women to try to move beyond the pain, grief and anger so quickly that they negate their mothers entirely. For these Denial Daughters, their life stories become, "I had a mother. She's dead. I've moved on." The result, however, is a kind of motherless martyrdom that puts the focus on absence. This lacking can taint the rest of their lives, creating an insatiable emotional need that they try to fill with other people, money, success, sex, food and other inadequate substitutes.

Living in a motherless martyrdom, we avoid the
memories that have the power to heal us.

For others, the pain of the lost relationship prevents them from remembering. These Suppression Sisters stay away from that emotional territory for fear the sadness will overwhelm them. They're embarrassed by their grief and concerned that their friends will judge them as depressed, weak or emotionally crippled. They avoid the very memories that have the power to heal them. They do not dare recall the mother who loved and nurtured them for fear that her absence from their day-to-day lives will be more than they can handle. So they are motherless in their lives and in their memories.

The Runaways believe that there is so much unfinished business with their mothers that they feel powerless. It's impossible, they tell themselves, to resolve a conflict with someone who had the nerve to die before they got this straightened out. Or else the anger they feel toward their mothers is so bitter that they suppress it out of guilt, remembering the old admonishment that one can't speak ill of the dead.

Breaking the Emotional Shackles

Most of us fit into more than one category of "mother denial," and some of us may find ourselves reflected partially in all of them. The good news is that healing and a release from our emotional shackles are possible. Answering the Call to Connection, we make a conscious decision as adults to get to know our mothers again. We begin from the place we left off: as daughters. But that is only the doorway to a deeper understanding.

On the Path of Understanding we stand as equals with our mothers. Woman to woman, we seek an understanding of the maternal forces in our lives. From that understanding comes healing. Where there is healing, there is love.

As we begin our journey to greater understanding,
the souls or spirits of our mothers become
willing partners on the path.

As daughters begin this journey, they quickly realize that they are not the only ones working to establish this connection. It is as if their mothers' spirits—or souls, or energy, or whatever terminology you are most comfortable with—become willing partners in these exercises. Coincidences, uncanny circumstances and surprise discoveries mark the way.

❦

Helen, a sensitive, introspective woman in her sixties, was cleaning out a closet in her sister's home in preparation for putting the house up for sale. As she sorted through various belongings, she came across a treasure that, in retrospect, seems a little miraculous. In a box on the top shelf of that closet were photographs of her mother that Helen had never seen before. The photographs reveal a woman that Helen did not know, an amazing find given the fact that her mother died fifty years ago when Helen was only sixteen.

The first portrait, taken before Helen was born, shows a beautiful, well-dressed woman seated near a fireplace with her three eldest children. The woman radiates a sense of contentment with her life and her children. In the second portrait, two-year-old Helen sits on her mother's lap, while her sisters stand to their mother's right and her brother on the left. Her mother looks straight into the camera, her dark eyes alive. With her refined features and a placid smile, she resembles a young Barbara Stanwyck.

"It was a real discovery," Helen says of the photographs. "I never thought of my mother as an attractive, sexy woman. My mother was so beautiful. That was a revelation."

This was a sharp contrast to the woman Helen remembered, the mother who had been sickly and bedridden with Parkinson's disease.

A Glimpse in the Mirror

The desire to get to know our mothers again may spring from a realization of how much we are like them. How often do we catch a glimpse of our own reflections in the mirror, surprised to discover our mother's expressions in our own? This realization often carries mixed emotions, since it challenges our notion of being individuals unlike anyone else, and perhaps evokes fears that we are somehow destined to make the same mistakes as our mothers. The truth is that by realizing how we are similar to our mothers and how we are decidedly different, we can operate from the strength that comes from self knowledge, as opposed to being steered by emotional forces under the surface. For many women, sharing a positive connection with their mothers is a source of comfort as they begin the search for deeper understanding.

Florence remembers being told by a family friend how much her voice and laugh were like her mother's. That comes as no surprise, since Florence is strongly connected with her mother through the oral traditions: Florence, a Mohawk Indian from the Iroquois Nation, is a professional storyteller and a motivational speaker. Her mother appeared frequently on public television programs on

Native American culture. Florence learned the old stories from her mother. When she shares them with her children or with an audience, she feels a deep connection with her mother as well as her grandmother, who helped raise her.

With such a strong connection it is little wonder that their Indian names are complementary—although it is only coincidence, since they were bestowed at different times by different people. Her mother was The Break of Dawn. Florence is The Rising Sun.

"I believe very firmly that we are a spiritual people," Florence says. "I firmly believe that my mother is in a much better place. But because we're only at this level of human experience with our five little senses, there is no way we can appreciate where she is."

Women from a variety of religious backgrounds and spiritual perspectives share the experience of an ongoing relationship with their deceased mothers.

Regardless of religious background or spiritual perspective, many women have a sense of their mother's spirits living on in some form or state of being. Some speak of heaven, others of a less defined spiritual existence. For some, their mothers live on in their memory. No matter what one's theology or philosophy, daughters experience an ongoing relationship because of the continued influence their deceased mothers exert on their lives. I am not speaking of a psychic influence in which our mothers directly touch our lives—although I don't rule it out, either. I'm speaking of memories and traditions, strengths and fears that we trace back to our mothers. We begin by acknowledging our mother's existence. It may sound basic, but many of us avoid the pain and grief by avoiding any connection with our mothers.

My sister, Bernadette, had a strong Call to Connection that made her realize she was in a state of denial of our mother's existence. Bernadette, a single mother who had gone back to college at the age of forty, received a notice in the mail that she had been chosen to receive a prestigious academic award of excellence. Along with the notice came a publicity card for the local newspaper. Filling out the essential information, Bernadette wrote "deceased" in the line for "mother's name" and started to fill out the next line. But she couldn't write another word.

"I realized that I was denying her existence," Bernadette explains.

She went back to that line and added her mother's name. It was a simple but powerful reminder for Bernadette that while her mother was dead, a connection between them remained. "I realized that, if Mother were alive, she'd be so proud of me," she adds.

From Daughters to Sisters

A deeper understanding of our
mothers requires us to stop being children,
to put aside some childhood issues that block
our understanding of our mothers.

On the journey to greater connection with our deceased mothers, we begin as daughters. But quickly we become sisters.

A deeper understanding of who our mothers were as women requires us to stop being children. This means deciding to put aside some of the childhood issues that may block our under-standing. They are often small, petty and even laughable. But until we unearth these issues, which often take the form of resentment, we can't move beyond the child role. It is essen-tial that we choose to put aside the facts that we were forced to wear hand-me-downs; couldn't shave our legs soon enough; were forbidden to date until long after our friends could; and never heard enough compliments and praise. To paraphrase St. Paul, "When I was a child, I spoke and thought and reasoned as a child does. But when I became an adult, my thoughts grew far beyond those of my childhood." We were our mothers' children; now we are their peers.

The first step in that shift is to look beyond what our moth-ers did to our understanding of who they were. It begins with a yes or no answer to the following question: Did your mother love you? The majority of women answer yes, although many of us want to qualify that with explanations of how our moth-ers did not love us enough or did not express their love in the way we wished. But the root answer for many of us is yes, our mothers loved us. We accept that as fact and use it as a plat-form to move on.

Focusing on the Essence

This is what author and intuitive Sonia Choquette calls focusing on our mother's "essence" and not her "process." For many of us, the essence of our relationship with our mothers is based on love. Our mothers loved us. How they expressed it—and whether they could express it at all—is an entirely different matter. But if love is the essence of a relationship, it is a powerful place to start.

For some daughters, the honest answer is no. They were abandoned or abused by their mothers, who through their own illnesses or addictions were unable to love and care for their daughters. Even in these cases, there is still a chance for healing, although it takes another form. The first step is to accept the reality of the relationship and the pain it caused. Pain acknowledged can be released, opening a daughter to the possibility of healing, and allowing love and nurturing to enter her life through other sources. We will more fully examine ways to heal the traumatic relationship in chapter 4.

While we acknowledge that our mothers loved us, many women feel this affection was not enough or not expressed in the way we needed. Many daughters also feel their mothers were unnecessarily critical of them, always pointing out their faults, from an extra five pounds to the way they raised their children.

As they pass on what they saw as good advice,
women are often hypercritical of themselves
and, by extension, of their daughters.

In most cases, I believe, our mother's criticism was rooted in two essential reasons. The first is that women are often hypercritical of themselves and, by extension, of their daughters. Our mothers often measured themselves as being lacking—in looks, intelligence, accomplishments or a host of other criteria. Many never considered themselves good enough for whatever prize they longed for, whether it was the love of their husbands or having children. For these women, everything seemed to be one crisis away from utter ruin and complete abandonment. That hypercriticism found another outlet in their daughters, the very mirrors of themselves and their lives. We had to be perfect in order to attain whatever prize our mothers held out for us.

Our mothers had our best intentions in mind when they pointed out what they saw as our faults. From the perspective of the women in my mother's generation, it was difficult for a woman to (a) get a good husband, (b) keep a good husband, (c) raise happy, obedient children, and (d) hold down a job that supported them. So in an effort to help us, they pointed out that we needed to lose weight, wear makeup, wear less makeup, never sleep with a man before marriage, insist the kids clean their plates, and for goodness sake learn to type even if you wanted to sing for a living.

Second, I believe there is an inherent competition in mother-daughter relationships, pitting the queen against the princess. Think of the fabled Electra complex, in which a girl becomes angry at her mother and attracted to her father. As a "daddy's girl" who was close to my father, I often found myself in competition with my mother for his attention. But most of us can stay angry at our mothers for just so long, or pull just so far away. We crave that maternal love and eventually begin to emulate our mothers.

For other women, conflicts arose out of the fact that we often had chances to realize our dreams more than our mothers did. Just think about the expanded choices for women today compared with the 1950s. Going back to our grandmothers' generation, think of the comparative personal, political and even sexual freedom among the suffragettes and flappers compared with the Victorian Gibson girls who preceded them. Some conflicts are generational, the understanding of which can heal a relationship.

Our mothers cannot love us perfectly.
That perfect unconditional love can
only come from God.

Allowing Our Mothers to Be Human

In all cases, we must realize that neither our mothers—nor anyone else, for that matter—can love us perfectly. It is damaging to ourselves and to them to expect it to be otherwise. The perfect unconditional love that fills us with a sense of wholeness and self-worth can only come from God, our Higher Power, the Universe or whatever terminology we are most comfortable with. While many of us from a Judeo-Christian background see God as male, the Creator encompasses both masculine and feminine. That perfect mother love can come only from God, whether we find that reflected in the feminine side of the Creator, through devotion to the Virgin Mary or through the Goddess tradition.

"We unfairly expect to get from our mothers the love that we need to get from the feminine face of God," explains Sonia Choquette, who as a psychic intuitive has counseled many women in their relationships with their mothers. "We look at our mother and demand, 'Why can't you be the heart of God?'"

With this perspective, everybody—mothers and daughters alike—gets the biggest break imaginable. Everybody gets to be human, without the unbearable and unrealistic burden of perfection.

※

Martha Borst knows the power of that perspective in her own life. As president of Phoenix 2000, Inc., which offers empowering personal growth seminars, she lives and teaches it.

"As people, we all seem to be on a journey to grow up, to become adults," Martha notes. "We stop expecting our parents to be the all-perfect gods and goddesses, the super-heroes and heroines. We realize that, at any point in time, our parents were men and women who were doing the best they knew how, no matter what they were like, given their upbringing and their conditioning."

Martha herself feels a strong bond with her deceased mother and, through meditation, feels her mother's warm and guiding presence. "For me, it's important to be in a loving space. I don't have any anger toward my mother or resentment," she says. "I feel total acceptance and forgiveness. I feel very clean with my mother."

We open ourselves to the possibility of
healing and of understanding our mothers and ourselves.
We allow our mothers into our lives once again,
seeking an ongoing connection with them.

Martha's relationship with her mother may seem ideal, leaving some of us to wonder if we'll ever reach that point. We only need to be open to the possibility of understanding and forgiving our mothers and ourselves. With an open mind and a clear intention toward healing and personal growth, we can let our mothers into our lives and actively seek a connection with them. It is nothing less than a rite of passage into full adulthood and equality with our mothers.

My mother was a strong woman, with very specific rules about what she viewed as right and wrong. There were times growing up when I was afraid of my mother, always trying to be the "good girl" to avoid her sharp tongue. Now, as a woman, I have to approach my mother and our relationship differently—from a place of strength and self-assurance. This is the only way I can get to know her without resentment standing in my way.

Our Mothers as Daughters

On the Path of Understanding, some women are lucky enough to have an invaluable map to guide them—diaries and journals written by their mothers years ago. On these pages, the women who were, or would later become, our mothers expressed their dreams and frustrations, anxiety and anger. The diaries often allow an intimacy that moves the reader from daughter to peer.

Cynthia has read the diaries her mother kept between the ages of fourteen and seventeen, chronicling her early teen years in the 1920s on a farm in Iowa, the move to the oil-boom town of Oklahoma City, the long train ride to a college near Boston and her career as a social worker in a women's prison in Massachusetts. The stories her mother relates—of dances and elocution lessons to refine the flapper girl, and the desire to have a meaningful career—allowed Cynthia to understand the brilliant, complex and emotionally dependent woman who was also her mother.

Reading the diaries now, some seventy years later, also has given Cynthia—who is pursuing an advanced degree in history—a remarkable sense of connection with her mother as a teenager. "As I read her diaries, I feel like I'm growing up all over again. Some of the phrases she uses, some of the things she says are things that I remember from my youth," Cynthia recalls.

Even if we do not have diaries and journals, we can still develop a sense of communication with our mothers. Links of word and image dwell within us, in our memories and in the stories that others tell us about ourselves and our mothers. Going forward, we also give voice to our sense of connection with our mothers, making it concrete by what we see, hear and say.

Talking to Mom

As I launched this book, I discussed the idea with my two sisters, who gave their enthusiastic support. I told my father, my aunts and then a few close friends. But the one person I did not "tell" right away was my mother. *If Mother were alive,* I thought, *she might not approve of me discussing our relationship openly.* In short, I was approaching her—and this book—from the perspective of the good girl trying to please. But as an adult woman empowered by her own choices, I could choose lovingly to undertake this project, in honor of my mother and all mothers and daughters everywhere.

One day, driving to pick up my son at preschool, I decided to tell Mother about the book. The car was a good place for this exercise, since I was alone and there was no chance of anyone overhearing me. A little self-conscious at first (and aware of the other drivers who might see me talking to myself), I spoke aloud of my desire to do this book project. I described my plans, hopes for the book and wider aspirations. I addressed my mother directly, hoping that she could hear me. I did not "hear" a reply, but I felt very clear about my intention to write this book. I had given myself permission, and in that felt her support as well.

Talking with your mother is one of the most powerful practices for establishing a continuing relationship with her. I do not pretend that my mother is still alive. But I do experience her presence, spiritually and psychologically, in my life. Some women may feel a little odd talking aloud to their deceased mothers, as I did at first. I simply suggest that you try it. Whether you picture yourself talking to your mother, to God, to your Higher Self or merely aloud, verbalizing thoughts, feelings and emotions is a very powerful exercise. Doing this, we literally give voice and therefore substance to them. It is the essence of what prayer is.

"Imagination is powerful," says Sister Mercedes Ventencilla, a missionary sister with the Columban Sisters and a former professor of theology at Centro Escolar University in Manila. "We can imagine our mothers here, face to face with us. If you were a clairvoyant, you could see your mother here. She is here because God is here."

Many women who feel a connection with their deceased mothers have told me they "talk" to them. These women do not consider themselves psychic or out of the mainstream at all. Two women, both in their fifties, told me separate stories of going to the cemetery to visit their mothers' graves and telling them of the latest news of the family. In one case, it was the engagement of a niece; in the other, the death of a brother.

"It's like a physical visit," says Janet, who goes to the cemetery regularly to talk to her mother. "I feel like I'm going to visit her."

❧

Betty, a gentle, religious woman with amazing physical and mental energy for her eighty-some years, confides that she speaks to her mother through prayer. "Sometimes I say, 'Lord, if possible, please tell my mother that I love her.'"

Now that she has reached old age as her mother did, Betty says she understands her mother's behaviors and attitudes. "I thought she was a pain in the neck sometimes," Betty laughs. "Now I understand that this was a natural part of getting older. I understand her so much more now."

---

*Forgiveness of our mothers does
not mean surrender.*

Seeking a greater connection with our mothers often involves forgiveness of their shortcomings and ours. But forgiveness does not mean surrender. It does not mean that it was okay to be criticized, belittled or abused. It means a line has been drawn, separating childhood and adulthood, and we have stepped over it.

Anger, hurt, frustration, jealousy, betrayal and a host of other emotions will be experienced and released during this journey. So will sadness and abandonment. But as part of the early steps to answer the Call to Connection, we lay down the ground rules. We approach the quest toward understanding as adults, nurturing the child inside as we move along. This is the only way to heal our pain, sorrow and anger that come from being the daughter of a deceased mother. It is the way out of the sorority of sadness that marks so many women.

As Reverend Janet Campbell of St. James Episcopal Church sees it, "It is important not to keep dragging the past into the present. We choose to begin the relationship anew."

We give ourselves permission to
explore our future as we lessen the hold
that the past has on us.

Forgive and Progress

By letting go of the past, we also allow ourselves to progress. No longer hindered by old wounds, we let go of the negative self-images that come from past hurts. We do not look at ourselves as shamed or inadequate. We are fully realized individuals with countless gifts and talents, many of which we have not yet dared to explore or express. Leaving the past behind, we give ourselves permission to explore the future unfettered by old baggage.

In her popular book, *Simple Abundance: A Daybook of Comfort and Joy*, Sarah Ban Breathnach writes of the need for women to explore within themselves to discover what she calls our authentic selves.

"Whether you realize it or not, you have lived many lives, and each one has left an indelible mark on your soul," she writes. "I'm not referring to reincarnation. I'm referring to the episodic way in which our lives evolve: childhood, adolescence, college years or early career, marriages, motherhood, perhaps life as single mother, widowhood and onward. . . . Each life experience leaves a layer of memory like a deposit of sediment: things we've loved and moments of contentment we've cherished that, when recalled, reveal glimmers of our true selves."

For those of us whose mothers have died, there is an extra layer of "sediment"—or maybe in this case it is "sentiment." We need to plow through the emotions surrounding the deaths of our mothers, through our childhoods and into the heart of the matter—the women who gave birth to us. In them we find the seeds of who we are—by imitation of or rebellion against. Knowledge of them is acknowledgment of ourselves.

Begin with a Memory

So how does one answer the Call to Connection? It begins with a memory and a quiet moment. Try to recall what your mother's voice sounded like, particularly how she said your name. For me, the only way I can imitate my mother's voice is to recall the deep, breathy way she said my nickname, "Trish": with a quick inhale before she spoke, and the "sh" drawn out for an extra second.

*Recall your mother's face, her voice,
her laugh. Recall how she said your name.*

Remember what your mother's face looked like. Study a photograph if you need to. Look into her eyes in the photo or in your imagination, and ask yourself what you see. Find a sample of her handwriting, a letter, a recipe or a birthday card you are now so grateful that you saved. It's tangible proof that she existed, even if there seems at the moment to be little connection between you.

Focusing on some tangible reminder, don't search for a particular memory. Let one rise. If it brings sadness, don't stop the memory or the feeling. Repressing both will only serve to block your emotions and deny you any connection with your mother at all. The feelings will pass and the memory will linger.

Examine the memory with your adult mind, not your child's perspective. Even if it is a bitter or angry memory, don't slip into the role of a small child. Stay an adult and reflect on what happened from that perspective. Here's an example from my own life.

❦

I remember being in the fourth grade and getting off the school bus just as a snowstorm hit. For some reason, my mother wasn't home when I arrived and, even though I knew where the key was, I didn't go in the house. Instead, I walked less than a quarter mile down the road to my grandparents' house to watch television with my cousins. My mother, skidding and sliding as she drove home as fast as she could, angrily discovered that I wasn't there. When she learned I was at my grandparents' house, Mother drove down to get me and buried the car in the quickly accumulating snow in my grandparents' driveway. She chewed me out in the car, venting her anger at me for going to my grandparents' in a snowstorm when I should have known she would be coming home any minute.

I used to tell the story from my nine-year-old perspective. Mean old Mama yelled at me for going to Grandma's in a snowstorm. But the adult in me takes a different view. My mother had the same emotional energy that I have, with a tendency toward high-highs and low-lows. A great source of conflict between Mother and me was our similarly quick tempers and sharp tongues. When I choose to view this incident as an adult, I see how stressed out she must have been to come home to an empty house, with three daughters and a husband out somewhere in a snowstorm.

Perhaps the memory that surfaces is a poignant one that underscores how much you miss your mother. Recalling the memory may bring tears to your eyes or a dull ache to your heart. But the pain passes, and what remains is a connective memory.

Sandy E., a bright and animated woman in her forties, recalls visiting her mother at the family home, a place she could walk into without knocking and without an invitation. After the deaths of her father and her mother, the family house was sold. While Sandy remains close to her siblings, none of their homes can take the place in her mind of her parents' house. From the adult perspective, however, Sandy makes an extra effort to maintain ties with her family and nurtures the connection with the mother by the re-creation of simple rituals. For Sandy, this includes baking cookies during the holidays from the same family recipes that her mother used.

"I do the baking for her. I feel I am her representative when I do that," Sandy explains.

Seek out shared activities that bring a sense of connection with your mother.

Activities that remind us of our mothers strengthen our link with them. For some, like Sandy, it's cooking. For others, it's gardening. My friend Janie, a news executive and writer in her early forties, connects with her mother when she shops—and has a beautiful wardrobe to prove it. "I guess my mother wanted me to have this," she jokes as she models an off-white silk blazer.

Clinical psychologist Dr. Patricia Garrity calls these positive connections "cherishable memories." They help us as daughters recall the nurturing presence of our mothers and carry that loving influence into our lives. It is a perspective that Dr. Garrity knows firsthand. For her, nurturing memories of her own mother revolve around their telephone calls to discuss an event or merely to check in. Whatever the reason, Dr. Garrity recalls, her mother was "always thrilled to hear from me."

Looking Beneath the Surface

Connective memories can be found even when, on the surface, our lives are vastly different from our mothers'. My own mother was a housewife who tended her home and gardens and cooked big meals every night. I am a journalist and writer, spending most of what passes for free time—usually before my son wakes up or after he has gone to sleep—at the keyboard. I take care of my own house, but not to the extent my mother did. Her floors were clean enough to eat off of; mine sometimes collect enough crumbs to make a meal.

Where Mother and I connect is the energy and daily patterns of our lives. She is the founder of what I call my theory of perpetual motion: If you keep moving, everything eventually gets done. Like my mother, I have a high energy level that is fueled at times by too much caffeine. As I sit at my keyboard at dawn on a Saturday, I remember how my mother often had the first load of wash on the clothesline while the dew was still on the grass. She had a funny, impulsively playful side that could make her irresistible. I remember one Halloween when Mother decided we were going out dressed up as mobsters in my father's old suits. My Italian-American relatives were quite amused. It is that spirit that draws me along the Path of Understanding.

The Love Connection

Our connection with our mothers may also be reflected in our other relationships. Many women speak of a closeness they share with siblings and other relatives through their efforts to talk about and better understand their mothers. In other cases, the loving relationships we allow into our lives reflect and honor the nurturing we received from our mothers. Our sense of having been loved by them gives us the confidence to seek and accept that love from another person.

❧

Mirah, an intelligent and vivacious teacher in her twenties, spoke to me just a few months before she married her fiancé, Jeff, whom she met a year after her mother died. Their attraction was mutual and instantaneous. She is convinced that, on some level, her mother helped bring them together.

"One day soon after we met, Jeff told me he heard this voice say to him, 'Take care of my baby.' That's just the kind of thing my mother would say," Mirah recalls. "My mom sent Jeff to me. With him, I have never been loved so tenderly in my life."

We build a portrait of our mothers through the memories and shared recollections of others in her life.

Connecting Through Memories

The Call to Connection begins inside ourselves, but quickly branches out to include others in our lives. We actively build a portrait of our mothers as women from a variety of perspectives. We speak to her peers, other family members and even our own friends who remember her. With each layer a more complex picture emerges, until our mothers appear as multi-faceted, multidimensional women with trials and triumphs, dreams and fears. They will seem contradictory and yet predictable, elusive yet easy to read. In short, they will be flesh and blood, reflecting more than just a little of who we are inside.

Memories are a gift. It is a huge mistake to bury this treasure chest. Talk about your mothers to a safe, discriminating audience. The clerk scanning your groceries may not find recollections of your childhood to be particularly fascinating. Neither will the more self-absorbed people in your life (you know who they are). But share memories with those who are closest to you. Siblings or other close relatives often enjoy a story you recall. Don't be surprised if they remember an incident differently than you did. Memories have a habit of becoming subjective. Don't give up your version of the story just because your brother recalls that Mom dented the fender of the Chrysler on the way to Niagara Falls and not Lake Placid. The more important thing is to share the memory and to laugh, if possible.

Sharing stories about our mothers with those who are closest to us also reveals another side of ourselves.

Talk about your mother to friends who want to know more about you. Listening to a particular anecdote, a friend is treated to a different side of you and the family you came from. Your friend may also provide a startling insight from an outsider's perspective that you never considered before.

The Call to Connection is real. It is the gentle tug to remember, sort out and understand. It holds the promise of healing of both ourselves and our relationships with our deceased mothers. But more important, it is a chance to connect with our mothers on a deeper, adult level—woman to woman. On that level of understanding we take our place among the generations of women that preceded us and lead the way for those that will follow us. For that is the higher, loftier purpose of answering the Call to Connection. Whether we are mothers or aunts, or simply touch the lives of our friends' children, our own healing extends a healthier bridge to the next generation.

Connections

The Call to Connection begins with a memory. Often repressed by pain, sadness, anger or guilt, memories need to be unlocked and savored. They hold the key to understanding our deceased mothers and seeing, as adults, the patterns that shaped our family lives. To start on this journey, it is essential to come to a loving place within oneself, to allow the memories to surface—and not just our usual stock of recollections that we sanitized in the retelling or intentionally reinterpreted for our own purposes. But pure memory, like a videotape stored in our subconscious minds, is a source of fresh information. For many women, these memories are accessed by action, doing things that we associate with our mothers.

Links to Your Mother

- Think of the activity that links you to your mother the most—perhaps an interest that you both share. Cooking? Gardening? Taking long walks? Shopping? Reading?

- Choose a day to undertake that activity in her memory. If it is cooking, prepare her signature meal (no need to compete anymore) and recall her special touches. If it is gardening, think of how she loved digging in the soil.

- Did your mother hum or sing while she worked in the garden or around the house? Did the two of you carry on a conversation while you worked? Do that now and don't be afraid to talk out loud to your mother. It helps release feelings that may have been bottled up for too long.

- If shopping is the activity that connects you to your mother, dress up a little for the occasion and treat yourself to something special. Observe the colors, textures and scents around you as you shop. Our senses evoke memories that our conscious minds may have forgotten.

We're on overload. Careers, houses, children, spouses, families and even our friends demand too much of us. We're too busy to think about what we're going to have for dinner tonight, let alone contemplate our past or our future. There simply isn't enough time. Living our lives at such a frenetic pace, it's no wonder we feel disconnected. Being too busy, however, is an all-too-convenient excuse we use to avoid the emotional issues of our lives.

We all employ it: the Denial Daughters who desperately seek to move on with their lives, the Suppression Sisters who avoid their feelings, the Runaways who have unfinished business with their mothers. Still, we feel a persistent tug at the core of our being, urging us to get in touch with ourselves. It is the Call to Connection, to get to know our mothers as women and, by extension, to discover the essence of ourselves. All it requires of us is to slow down for a moment and listen.

The Meditative Moment

- Meditation or a quiet moment allows memories to drift through our conscious minds. If you are given to meditation, use it to free your mind to contemplate your relationship with your mother.

- Try journal writing, as I do, to delve into your thoughts and memories.

- Let your mind wander when you are performing a mundane task like vacuuming or relaxing in the bathtub. When our frantic minds are quiet enough, we allow ourselves to contemplate. In whatever manner works for you, give your mind some quiet time to reflect and remember.

After Mother died, I inherited a beautiful bracelet that Dad gave her one Christmas. It is so lovely—links of gold with a filigree edge and five small diamonds in the center. I wore it twice in ten years: once on my wedding day and once for a formal business dinner. Now, after establishing a deeper connection with my mother, I wear that bracelet frequently as a physical connection to my mother. Equally important, I also wear that bracelet as a celebration of my own femininity. In that spirit, I have found a deep connection with my mother.

The Clothing Connection

- Wear a piece of your mother's clothing or jewelry, if possible.
- If what you choose is particularly beautiful or was treasured by your mother, wear it as an adult woman honoring her own femininity, not as a little girl playing dress-up.
- Carry with you a letter or a recipe that she had written. Women are sensitive to touch, making physical proximity to something of your mother's a powerful link.

Taking my son to the park one day, I brought my mother along. As Patrick pedaled his blue tricycle down the sidewalk, I envisioned my mother walking with me. I imagined how she would chatter with Patrick, as I was doing, along the way.

I could feel how much she would enjoy that walk to the park, in the company of one of her daughters and her grandson. That is the essence of the Mother Walk. This exercise of envisioning your mother in your present life can be done anywhere and anytime. For me, I enjoy the Mother Walk on the way to the park. But it's possible to employ the Mother Walk meditation in the garden, in the car, at the beach or in the cemetery. Our imaginations are powerful tools, helping us to envision our mothers' physical presence in our lives. By inviting them in, we remember the nurturing we received, feel the connection in the activities we enjoyed, and begin a healing of old hurts and resentments.

The Chat Corner / The Mother Walk

- Begin a dialogue with your mother. This may feel a little awkward at first, but try it in a private moment while driving alone, or gardening, or during any other solitary activity. Tell her you want to get to know her again. Tell her you seek to understand her as a woman.

- Stating your intention aloud makes it real—to yourself. Once you are clear about this journey, your subconscious mind will cooperate. Answers within yourself will become more accessible to you.

- Take a Mother Walk. Stroll through your neighborhood, down a country road, along a beach or any other quiet place, and envision your mother walking beside you. Imagine what she would say and the observations she would make. If in your mind your mother becomes critical or negative, firmly tell her that this is no longer allowed. Envision her from the perspective of the loving and nurturing that you received.

- Set aside a time—once a week, once a month—and a special place for the Mother Walk. Try different venues for this meditative practice such as the garden, the cemetery, your car, your home, or even the shopping mall.

- If you feel anger or resentment toward your mother, talk to her while undertaking a physical activity like raking leaves or hauling the trash from the garage. That will help channel the anger into energy you can expend.

Remember and reflect. Meditate, journal and pray. Look within yourself to find the key to your mother and yourself. It's all there, waiting to be discovered.

READER/CUSTOMER CARE SURVEY

HEFG

We care about your opinions! Please take a moment to fill out our online Reader Survey at **http://survey.hcibooks.com**. As a **"THANK YOU"** you will receive a **VALUABLE INSTANT COUPON** towards future book purchases as well as a **SPECIAL GIFT** available only online! Or, you may mail this card back to us and we will send you a copy of our exciting catalog with your valuable coupon inside.

(PLEASE PRINT IN ALL CAPS)

First Name		MI.		Last Name	

Address				City	

State		Zip		Email	

1. Gender
- ☐ Female   ☐ Male

2. Age
- ☐ 8 or younger
- ☐ 9-12   ☐ 13-16
- ☐ 17-20   ☐ 21-30
- ☐ 31+

3. Did you receive this book as a gift?
- ☐ Yes   ☐ No

4. Annual Household Income
- ☐ under $25,000
- ☐ $25,000 - $34,999
- ☐ $35,000 - $49,999
- ☐ $50,000 - $74,999
- ☐ over $75,000

5. What are the ages of the children living in your house?
- ☐ 0 - 14   ☐ 15+

6. Marital Status
- ☐ Single
- ☐ Married
- ☐ Divorced
- ☐ Widowed

7. How did you find out about the book?
(please choose one)
- ☐ Recommendation
- ☐ Store Display
- ☐ Online
- ☐ Catalog/Mailing
- ☐ Interview/Review

8. Where do you usually buy books?
(please choose one)
- ☐ Bookstore
- ☐ Online
- ☐ Book Club/Mail Order
- ☐ Price Club (Sam's Club, Costco's, etc.)
- ☐ Retail Store (Target, Wal-Mart, etc.)

9. What subject do you enjoy reading about the most?
(please choose one)
- ☐ Parenting/Family
- ☐ Relationships
- ☐ Recovery/Addictions
- ☐ Health/Nutrition
- ☐ Christianity
- ☐ Spirituality/Inspiration
- ☐ Business Self-help
- ☐ Women's Issues
- ☐ Sports

10. What attracts you most to a book?
(please choose one)
- ☐ Title
- ☐ Cover Design
- ☐ Author
- ☐ Content

FOLD HERE

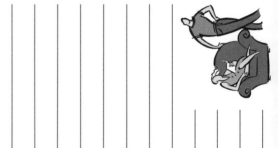

Comments

2

Beyond the Grief

There is a time for everything:
a time to be born, a time to die; a time to plant,
a time to harvest; a time to kill, a time to heal;
a time to destroy, a time to rebuild; a time to cry,
a time to laugh; a time to grieve,
a time to dance. . . .

—ECCLESIASTES 3:1–4

*W*hen we were born, the umbilical cord that connected our infant bodies to our mothers was cut.
When our mothers died, another tie was severed: that of the
day-to-day relationship between parent and child. While a
connection, psychological or spiritual, remains after a
mother's death, a daughter experiences a fundamental change
in her life. There are no more phone calls; shopping trips;
Mom's cooking; criticism of bad haircuts, too-red lipstick or

wild boyfriends; or comments about one's choice of a spouse or the raising of children.

It's no wonder, then, that the death of a mother unleashes such conflicting emotions.

Mother-daughter relationships are by nature complex, a mixture of conflict and closeness that is rarely seen in any other human bond. Our mothers are the source of our life, regardless of what happens later. We literally inhabit her for months, then spend a lifetime separating from her. We seek to define where she leaves off and we begin. This come-close, pull-away dynamic is common in many mother-daughter relationships. We find ourselves reflected in her and she in us, while at the same time establishing our autonomy. The mother-daughter link is so basic, so primal, nothing can fully replicate it.

"No matter how much your husband loves you or you experience the love of children, no one loves you like your mother," observes Barbara, a professional woman in New York whose mother died within the year before she made this statement.

Locked in Time

When it comes to our relationships with our deceased mothers, many of us are locked in an emotional time warp. Regardless of how far we've come in other areas of our lives, personal or professional, our relationships with our mothers are the same now as they were at the time of our mothers' deaths.

A daughter's attitude toward her mother's death, says Dr. Joyce Fraser, a psychologist in St. Claire Shores, Michigan, reflects where she is emotionally at that time in her life. Daughters who are "less evolved" in their relationships with the mothers see the world through the "prism of their own needs," she adds. Often these daughters are very angry over their mothers' deaths, which they may view as abandonment. "Who is going to take care of me?" they ask themselves and the world. "Why did you leave me?" In a more evolved mother-daughter relationship, the death is viewed more as a natural part of the life cycle, even though these daughters still grieve the loss.

Unless we work on issues with our mothers that remain after their deaths, we can be trapped in an emotional suspended animation. In this context, a woman in her fifties, with a career, family and home of her own, may feel very much like a wounded adolescent when she contemplates the mother who died when she was twelve years old. In my own case, until I embarked on the Path of Understanding, I remained where I was in my relationship with my mother when she died: a twenty-six-year-old, fighting to establish my own identity and struggling with what I perceived were her expectations. In order to move forward, I had to take emotional stock of the relationship as it existed *at that moment*.

Acknowledging our feelings without judgment is the only way to free ourselves.

The death of a mother unleashes a full gamut of emotions, from pain and grief to fear and resentment. The problem, especially years after a mother's death, is that we can easily find a dozen reasons not to explore those feelings. Once the sharp edge of pain has been dulled, few of us want to remember how bad we felt. We don't want to be reminded of how much we miss the woman who gave birth to us or who, over the years, had become a friend and companion.

And we certainly don't want to contemplate how down-to-the-bone, raw-nerved, white-hot angry we were with her at times. We may feel uncomfortable admitting, even to ourselves, that we had conflicts with our deceased mothers. We would rather focus on the good memories and forget about everything else. But that "other stuff"—anger, fear, resentment—can't just be forgotten. It has to be healed. To do that, we must first be honest with ourselves about our relationships with our mothers. More than likely, it was not perfect. There were probably conflicts and hurt feelings on both sides, rivalry, and criticism that was perceived as unfair.

"Sure I miss my mother," confides Lisa, a writer and journalist with a sharp mind and a razor wit. "But I don't miss all of her."

Lisa recalls the intelligent, involved woman who was her mother, the one with whom she enjoyed discussing world events. But she also remembers her mother's sharp criticism and scanty praise. "She would look at my report card—all A's and one B—and say, 'What about this B?' She wouldn't even comment on the A's."

Emotional Signposts

The feelings that linger after a mother's death are powerful signposts on the Path of Understanding. These feelings point out the healing that is needed in our lives as we discover anew our mothers' identities as women. If the thoughts of our mothers bring up a deep sadness because we miss their companionship, we need to bring their spirit, or essence, into our lives again. If we feel bitter anger or resentment, we need to own those feelings, instead of "stuffing" them away. Allowing ourselves to feel those negative emotions that sometimes scare us or make us feel ashamed, we give ourselves permission to heal as we explore the roots of the conflicts with our mothers.

Whatever our feelings surrounding the deaths of our mothers, it is time to unearth and acknowledge them. Grief, anger, resentment—these emotions can be turned into energy to propel us along the Path of Understanding.

For some of us, our feelings surrounding our mothers' deaths are near the surface and easily accessible. For others, they have been buried. We blocked our feelings of pain, grief, abandonment, liberation or whatever else we felt when our mothers died because we simply could not deal with these emotions at the time. We learned to anesthetize ourselves as a means of coping and going on with our lives.

We became the Denial Daughters, pretending everything was just fine. We became the Suppression Sisters, stuffing our feelings away.

After our mothers died, it seemed friends were so eager for us to get on with our own lives that we became the Denial Daughters, pretending everything was just fine. Or we joined the Suppression Sisters, so concerned about our children, our spouses, our siblings and our friends, that we stuffed our feelings away. Sometimes our own feelings frightened us. *Why do*

I still feel sad? we asked ourselves. *Am I really depressed or is this normal?* We were so eager to stop feeling awful that we pretended we were okay. The denial and the suppression became patterns and, years later, we don't know how we feel about our mothers anymore. But every time we see a Hallmark card commercial for Mother's Day, we alternate between wanting to dissolve into tears or throw a shoe through the television screen.

The Intersection of Guilt and Anger

Guilt and anger: these two emotions seem to go together. We feel guilty about being angry at our mothers, and angry at ourselves for feeling guilty. We feel guilty for all the times we didn't go visit our mothers and blame ourselves for every argument we ever had. We impose guilt on ourselves for what we believe we should have done when our mothers were alive.

Sandy K., who grew up in a large Italian-American family in Chicago, recalls the pull she felt between her dying mother and her two daughters, one an infant and one a toddler. "When I was with my mother, I wanted to be with my daughters. When I was with my daughters, I wanted to be with my mother."

Anger burns at the edges as we contemplate the litany of "why" questions that often revolve around the mother-daughter relationship: *Why did she act this way? Why did she criticize me? Why didn't she show me that she loved me? Why wasn't she there for me?*

Becoming a Runaway to forget the past, we risk obliterating the positive nurturing we received.

So why not just chuck it all and start fresh? Become a Runaway, and forget the past and start again? Because if we try to clean the slate in hopes of obliterating any pain from the past, we will also erase whatever positive mothering and nurturing we received. Going forward, we choose to develop a healthy, ongoing connection with our mothers from a place of understanding.

Understanding our mothers' lives also gives us unparalleled freedom to become who we are, who we choose to become.

"I really mark the beginning of my journey toward being a healthy woman with my mother's death," says novelist Joyce Maynard, herself the mother of three. Her mother's death, Joyce explains, was a catalyst to examine not only her mother's life but her own. What Joyce found was that she loved her mother deeply and was proud of her—a writer who wrote "voluminously" and had a Ph.D., which was rare for women of her era. But what Joyce also discovered was that her mother had failed to give her a blueprint for living life as a healthy, fulfilled woman.

"She was such a super-mother, so self-sacrificing," Joyce explains. "She would do anything for her daughters."

Joyce's mother—like Joyce herself—endured a lonely, unhappy marriage. Her mother finally divorced after Joyce and her sister were grown. Joyce, on the other hand, ended her marriage even though her children were young. At about the same time her mother died. It was an act of independence that declared she was taking charge of her life for her sake and that of her children.

"I am one of a long line of mother's daughters, and I'm fighting to change the pattern," Joyce explains. "I don't want my daughter to feel the kind of guilt and obligations that I had."

On the Life Cycle

Issues with our mothers will surface at various times of our lives. A marriage or birth of a child may make us miss our mothers acutely, or make us feel angry and abandoned that they are not here to help. Divorce, illness, or the death of a friend or loved one may bring up sadness and mourning that stem from the time our mothers passed away. Often these issues catch us off guard, confronting us with conflicting and perplexing emotions.

Looking beyond the surface, however, we can often trace these feelings back to our relationships with our mothers. Once we acknowledge that these issues will continue throughout our lives, we no longer fear them. In fact, they serve as powerful reminders to how important our link is to our mothers and how deep the need is to connect with them again.

So how do we go about unearthing the emotions surrounding our mothers' deaths? For some women, the process will be fairly easy. Their relationships with their mothers were straightforward. Any conflicts between mother and daughter had already been resolved. For these daughters, the Mourners, emotions may be close to the surface.

Chances are, the emotions surrounding our relationships with our mothers are the ones that have been playing out in our lives.

For others—the Denial Daughters, Suppression Sisters and Runaways—it will require a little more work and a lot of honesty. But chances are, the emotions that we have hidden or denied are the ones that have been playing out in our lives since that time. If we felt abandoned by our mothers, we may have difficulty believing that everyone else in our life won't suddenly leave us bereft. Or we may feel so vulnerable that we don't let people get too close to us. Unaddressed anger and unacknowledged sadness may result in our lashing out at people for no apparent reason. Even the most sweet-tempered woman, out of touch with how much she misses her mother, may feel a deep jealousy for her friends whose mothers are still alive.

While shopping once, Sandy E. overheard a woman calling across the clothing racks to her mother. "I thought, *Why does she get to have a mother and I don't?* I had to leave the store."

Or maybe, underneath it all, there is just a touch of liberation. No more competition. No more feeling not good enough. No more criticism. The queen is dead, long live the queen.

There are no right or wrong feelings, despite what we or our relatives would like to believe.

When a Daughter Is Young

What we daughters experience when our mothers die depends largely on our age and how we viewed the world at that time.

If our mothers died when we were infants or toddlers, there is likely to be no conscious memory. We know today that babies hear and respond to some stimuli in the womb, but most of us cannot recall that time (although some women have undergone regression and re-birthing therapy, which, some people believe, puts them in touch with this early connection).

Our grief may come from not having had a chance to know our mothers, even though we had stepmothers, grandmothers, aunts or other nurturing women in our lives. We may feel abandoned by our mothers, even though intellectually we know this is not the case.

To heal, we need to seek a connection with our birth mothers by discovering who they were as women. We piece together stories told to us by others, compiling the knowledge of those who knew our mothers. As we get to know our mother, she will become real to us.

Doris, a retired schoolteacher, was only eight days old when her mother died of a heart condition. Now in her seventies, Doris still has a strong spiritual connection with her mother, reinforced by the portrait of her mother that sits on Doris's dresser. At first glance, the likeness between Doris and the mother she never knew is astounding. Beyond appearances, Doris's connection to her mother springs from a story that was related to her over the years. Her mother lost consciousness soon after Doris was born. But even unconscious and near death, it was clear that her mother was still aware of the baby girl she had just given birth to. Doris's mother regained consciousness for a short while, just long enough to inquire, "How is Marian Doris?" That's all she said, and with that the baby girl was promptly named.

Women who were young children when their mothers died may search for similarities that make their mothers seem more real to them. At the same time, they may be dealing with feelings of loss, grief, abandonment and anger that have their roots in childhood. As youngsters, we may have been distracted to keep from feeling our pain or exhorted "to be a big girl now" and not to cry. Adults may very well have underestimated our grief, believing that we could not comprehend what had happened. Now, as adults, we daughters may experience deep emotions of pain, anger, abandonment and guilt.

Madonna, the singer, dancer, actress and pop icon, was five when her mother passed away. An interviewer for *Vanity Fair* magazine makes this observation: "When her mother died of breast cancer, the disease was still treated by almost everyone as an unspeakable horror. Madonna understood little about what was happening except that her mother was gone. There was no good-bye, and perhaps she was left with feelings so big that they had to be buried, run away from."

When *Vanity Fair* asked Madonna about her mother, the performer replied, "I was told that my mother was very musical, and that she loved to dance, and that was that. She was into being a mother, but that doesn't mean you can't have an artistic soul. I'm sure she did, but not in any ambitious way."

Where mother stopped, daughter took off.

---

*As teenagers, experiencing the death of a parent
makes us suddenly so different from our peers.*

Those of us who were teenagers when our mothers died may also experience guilt for the rebellion that comes with being a teenager, and anger for suddenly being put into a position that makes us so different from our peers. We may have been the first among our classmates and friends to lose a parent, which made us feel strangely isolated, even though others seemed sympathetic. The problem is that we felt no one could possibly understand us, since they had not experienced the same profound loss. I came across a letter posted on the Internet recently, in which a teenage girl expresses the loneliness she feels after the death of her mother.

". . . I feel like I have no one to talk to. I see the school grief counselor once every three to four weeks, but I was wondering if there is any thing [sic] else that I might be able to do to lessen my feelings of depression and the feeling that I've been abandoned," the girl writes.

We daughters who were young when our mothers died may seek to re-create what we lost by having a baby early in life. When Mirah, at eighteen, learned that her mother was dying, she fought the urge to "go out and get pregnant."

"I wanted to share the experience of having a child with my mother," she says. "I knew I wouldn't have it later on." She made the decision not to have a baby until later in her life, but the emotional pull of motherhood remained strong.

As adult women, years and perhaps decades after our mothers' deaths, we must acknowledge the loss, guilt and abandonment. Then we seek to release ourselves from those feelings by actively pursuing the psychological and spiritual connections that link us to our mothers. By talking to people who knew our mothers when they were the ages we are now, we will get to know our mothers in a different way. We discover the ways in which we are both amazingly alike and decidedly different.

A Mother's Death, a Daughter's Youth

Even as adults, those of us who were young when our mothers died may feel a sense of outrage at being robbed of our youth. The deaths of our mothers forced us to grow up. In some cases, we may have had to help run a household or care for younger children long before we were ready. We may have stepped into the role of the "woman of the house" before we could come to terms with the loss of our mothers.

Decades ago, we did not have grief counselors to help us sort through our feelings. In fact, we may have become Suppression Sisters who denied our feelings to be "good girls," to help out the family. Resentment may run very deep.

That resentment, however, reflects the anger we feel toward our mothers for dying and our families who, consciously or not, made us the responsible ones. Healing begins when we decide to no longer be the martyr, a role that our families may be very tired of us playing. As we begin to connect with our mothers, we vow to give to ourselves the gift of our lost youth. What was it that we missed out on when we were teenagers? Was it going out with our girlfriends on a Saturday night because we had younger siblings to care for? Was it loss of a carefree attitude that so many of our friends had? Give it back to yourself now. Yes, you *can* go see a movie with three girlfriends on a Friday night. Your house and your family will still be there on Saturday morning.

The Two Camps of Adult Daughters

*Women may have unfinished business with their mothers,
issues that only the two of them can address.*

The Runaways

For those of us who were adults when our mothers died,
there appear to be two camps. Some of us may be Runaways
with unfinished business with our mothers, issues and conflicts
that were never resolved. Out of pain, sadness, guilt or anger
over our mothers' deaths, we may not even be fully aware of
those conflicts. But all we daughters need to do is stop to consider the emotional themes that run in our lives: abandonment, self-criticism, feeling unloved.

I have heard so many stories of very successful women who,
even in their forties and fifties, still wonder what their mothers would have thought of them. The perception of a mother's
judgment is a heavy burden to carry through life.

The healing comes by acknowledging the feelings and
learning to understand the dynamics of our mother-daughter
relationships from the perspective of mature, self-actualized
women. As we get to know our mothers again, we will learn
what made them tick. Their personalities, the context of their
lives, and the forces that shaped them will become more real
to us. Understanding our mothers as women, we will see them
in a new way, shedding light on the causes of the conflicts and
resentments.

There may be another, deeper reason many of us became
Runaways. If we never examine the conflicts and complexities

of our relationships with our mothers, we can avoid core issues in our own lives. We keep up the fronts and the barriers, the pretenses and the excuses, never looking too deeply into our love lives and careers, our dreams and self-esteem. But inevitably there comes a day when we can no longer hide, when we run out of self-negating disguises or admit our lives are no longer functional. We come face to face with ourselves and our beginnings.

Gilda, a musician, entertainer and budding writer at the age of sixty-nine, has delved relentlessly into her own life and her roots. She is trying to learn more about her mother, who was born in a *shtetl*, or ghetto, outside Kiev, Russia, in 1901. Gilda has written stories and sketches of her life entitled "Who Am I?" It is a question she keeps asking, as she looks deeper into her life and into her complex and often difficult relationship with her mother.

"I am the ten-year-old girl who stopped brushing her teeth in rebellion against her mother's note posted near her toothbrush, 'Have you brushed your teeth?' The girl who sat on the bedspread on which there was a note saying, 'Don't sit on the bedspread,'" Gilda writes.

The "Who Am I?" sketches span from her earliest memories at the age of three to the present moment. Gilda keeps looking for answers in her life to the key question of her identity.

The Mourners

The other group of adult daughters, the Mourners, grieve the loss of the ongoing day-to-day relationship with their mothers. For Mourners, conflicts more than likely were worked out when their mothers were alive. Often with their own homes, families and careers, Mourners experienced their mothers as women they came to enjoy as equals. With the death of their mothers came the loss of a friend's company.

❦

"She was such fun; I wish that God had let her stay around a little longer," Denise, an executive in her fifties, says with a smile.

A young widow who raised two children on her own, Denise's mother was a "late bloomer"—a phrase that Denise uses to describe herself. She supported her family and herself by working as a secretary well past the page of seventy. After retirement, she led an active life and traveled to Ireland, her ancestral homeland. But illness and old age took their toll, and Denise and her brother began to take more responsibility for their mother's day-to-day affairs.

"Sometimes when I'm out shopping and I see a woman with her white-haired mother, I want to say to that daughter, 'Cherish these times. They are precious,'" Denise says.

❦

Lisel Mueller, the Pulitzer Prize-winning poet, says she does not feel her relationship with her mother has really changed since her death, except that she misses and remembers her. "She was my friend from childhood on, always allowing and trusting me to be independent and go my own way, and we never had the conflicts of adolescence that so many mothers and daughters experience," Ms. Mueller wrote in a letter to me. She then referred me to a poem she wrote about her mother:

> I bring my mother back to life,
> her eyes still green, still laughing,
> She is still not fashionably thin.

She looks past me
for the girl
she left her old age to.
She does not recognize her
in me, a graying woman
older than she will ever be.

How strange that in the garden
of memory where she lives
nothing ever changes;
the heavy fruit
cannot pull the branches
any closer to the ground.

"THE GARDEN," FROM *ALIVE TOGETHER* BY LISEL MUELLER
PUBLISHED BY LOUISIANA STATE UNIVERSITY PRESS

Mourner daughters also may experience a sense of regret for the plans that, after our mothers' deaths, remain unfulfilled. After the birth of her second daughter, Sandy K. decided not to work outside the home any longer. Her plan was to devote herself to her daughters and to spend more time with her mother. While she stayed at home with her daughters, Sandy never had the chance to spend the leisure time with her mother that she had hoped for. When Sandy's second daughter was still an infant, her mother became ill. Three months later, she died.

"I felt I was robbed," Sandy explains. "I finally was at a point when I didn't have to work. I was looking forward to having time to spend with my mother and to share my children with her. But that didn't happen."

By bringing our mothers' spirits, or essence, into our lives, we alleviate the sense of loss and sadness. Instead of avoiding our mothers' memories, we actively cultivate them to give us a continuing sense of who our mothers were. We undertake certain activities—cooking, shopping, gardening, visiting a museum—in their memories. As with the Mother Walk, we seek to feel the connections with them.

Daughters who lost their mothers to old age or prolonged illness may feel the death was a blessed end. In these instances, our mothers' deaths literally released both of us. But often we faced a prolonged period of grieving, beginning with the shift in the mother-daughter roles. Illness or incapacity forced us to become mothers to our own parent. Our mothers, unable to care for themselves, became our children.

"I lost my mothering," Jean explains, "before I lost my mother."

Recalling the mothering we did receive is a
powerful way to make up for the loss.

By recalling the mothering we did receive, we bring this nurturing back into our lives. We remember what our mothers did for us that made us feel special or cherished, whether it was making us homemade soup or drying our mittens on the register overnight so our fingers would be warm on the way to school. We recall that mothering by performing nurturing tasks for ourselves and others in our lives.

A New Freedom

From a perspective of honesty, we can contemplate the relationships we had with our mothers with a new freedom. No

longer bound by family obligations or distracted by petty conflicts, we can look at our mothers with fresh eyes. More important, we no longer have to worry about our mothers' feelings
since they are no longer bound by their humanity. For those of
us who believe in a spiritual afterlife, there is the belief that our
mothers are perfected in their union with God. In that, our
relationships with our mothers can lead to spiritual healing. For
those of us who see a psychological connection with our mothers, healing comes when we acknowledge our true feelings.

Once uncovered, the feelings must be expressed. For me,
writing was the best way. Writing honored my feelings, making them legitimate. It also helped me to release them from
deep within myself. Once I had down on paper what I felt, I
could choose to move on. I was free to make the shift out of
motherlessness into a self-empowerment and self-love where I
could choose to explore the ongoing relationship with my
mother. I wrote, for my own benefit, my recollections of the
days before she died and my own feelings at her passing.

A Letter to Mom

Once I was in touch with my feelings, I had to let my
mother know. So I wrote her a letter on plain, legal-sized
paper. I wrote out my honest thoughts and feelings about her
and our relationship. I acknowledged a conflict that existed
long before her death and spoke of my understanding of it
now. I told her I loved her and asked her to pray for all of us.
I told her about her grandson. I tore the paper into small
pieces and put them in a bowl. In front of an open window, I
set fire to the paper and turned my thoughts and feelings into
energy. I felt the heat from the flame and smelled the smoke.
My spiritual e-mail was sent.

A large crow sat on the telephone pole in the back yard, cawing loudly to me as I fanned the smoke out the window. Perhaps it was greeting the sun that had turned the sky a pale pink on that summer morning. But the flash of gleaming black feathers and the raspy call triggered a memory I had nearly forgotten. As my letter burned, I remembered the three crows that were always in the back yard each morning when I was growing up. My mother, an early riser as I am, yelled out to those crows every morning as she opened the window to let in the morning breeze. "Good morning, crows," she'd call out. It was a funny little ritual.

It is a fanciful thought, but it seems appropriate that a crow witnessed my letter-burning ceremony that morning. Perhaps it was letting me know that Mother got the letter. Or maybe it was just adding its comments to mine.

---

*Expressing our feelings on paper,
we move emotional blocks that prevent us from
feeling a connection with our mothers
and others in our lives.*

Committing our feelings to paper helps us to sort out our emotions. Expressing what we are feeling, exactly as we experience it, helps us remove emotional blocks that keep us from feeling an ongoing connection with our mothers. Those blocks may also be preventing us from fully living our lives and connecting with others. Until we honor our own feelings, we will not be able to comprehend what others in our families are experiencing.

The Family System

As we get to know our mothers as women, seeing them as individuals, we will begin to view our families in a different light. But first, we must acknowledge the changes that our mothers' deaths have wrought in our families. We may feel closer to our siblings or more distant. We may sense the hub of the family wheel is missing and the spokes are flying off in different directions. We worry about Dad but, caught up in our own mother-daughter issues, do not have the emotional reserves to help him. Conflicts and competition suddenly surface or become exacerbated. Fingers of accusation point in all directions. We aren't grieving enough or we can't get over it. We aren't doing our share with Dad or we're keeping the others away from him. We're only concerned about the money or we won't face the reality of dealing with an estate.

When it comes to relationships with our mothers, competition among siblings is often acute. Somebody is deemed to be the favorite and another the black sheep. One can do no wrong, one can do nothing right. Someone is closer to Mom, another to Dad. But we do not always agree on who gets what designation.

Siblings in the same family
often experience uniquely different
relationships with their mother.

In doing research for this book, I talked separately with sisters about their deceased mothers. One conclusion I reached quickly, and saw reflected in myself and my two sisters, is that each mother-daughter relationship is unique. For every child, there seems to have been a separate mother. When those different mothers don't match up, sibling rivalry flares.

As we get in touch with our feelings and establish a connection with our mothers, it is important that we respect our siblings' views. No one's emotions are right or wrong. There doesn't have to be a consensus on perceptions. Each of us experienced a one-on-one relationship with our mothers, regardless of how many children there are in our families. Although our thoughts, feelings and insights may be shared with our siblings, our perceptions cannot be imposed as "truth" in such an emotional arena.

One reason for the different perceptions is that in life, our mothers had very unique relationships with us. As the youngest of three sisters, I experienced my mother differently from what my sisters did. Not better or worse, just differently. While I have no brothers to gauge personal experience, many women who do say the sisters were treated differently from the brothers. Often, women view their brothers as having been their mothers' favorites.

Daughters and Sons

In church one Sunday, I overheard two women talking about this very subject. While I don't usually give in to eavesdropping, the insight they shared was so powerful, I couldn't help but listen in.

"You know, the relationship between a mother and a son is so different," one of the women said. "I love my daughters, but my relationship with my son is different. I think that bothers my daughters sometimes."

A daughter's perception of and relationship
with her mother is often vastly different
from what her brother experiences.

Unlike a son, a daughter may sense a competition with her mother. Or she may be the target of her mother's criticism, which is often an extension of the mother's harsh view of herself. On the positive side, mothers and daughters can enjoy an intimacy in our culture far longer than mothers and sons. Daughters may be physically affectionate with their mothers longer than sons. On balance, the relationships experienced by sons and daughters are vastly different. Understanding and acknowledging that difference can lead to a healing not only between mother and daughter, but between sister and brother as well.

"I always felt my mother loved my brother more than me," admits Lois, an education professional in her late fifties. The reason, Lois explains, is that her mother and her brother had the same strong, dominant personality, while Lois and her father were both emotional "softies."

But as Lois matured and had a family of her own, she gained insight into her mother's personality. Echoing an experience common to many women, Lois says, "I came to understand my mother when I became a mother myself."

She saw that her mother had difficulty expressing her emotions, even stoically bearing the sorrow of Lois's father's death. "The one time I saw her cry was when she had shingles, which were very painful. Maybe it was that Russian character; they were strong and powerful." Lois's mother was born in Russia and had emigrated to the United States as a small child with her family.

A rabbi who spoke at her mother's funeral summed it all up for Lois, using the analogy of the sabra cactus fruit that is native to Israel. "He said my mother was like the sabra fruit," said Lois, "hard on the outside and soft on the inside."

The Family Power Shift

In many families, mothers are the power center. They are the clearinghouse for information, the source of family knowledge and a font of ready opinion. When our mothers die, those roles are suddenly up for grabs, even if our fathers are still alive.

"We rarely talked to each other. Our mother kept us informed with what was happening in each other's lives," Lisa explains. "After she died, we had to learn to communicate with each other. That's been especially difficult with my brothers, trying to get them involved in our lives."

Some of us step into the mother role—regardless of our age or that of our siblings. We may try to become everyone's caregiver, often at the expense of our own needs. This martyr's role may be our way to suppress our own feelings as we try to lose ourselves in everyone's else problems. Others of us may distance ourselves from the family, an action that may spark resentment among our siblings. But what looks like coldness on the surface may simply be our defense mechanism against the pain and grief.

Our relationships with our fathers change. He may suddenly need more emotional support from his children than before, or he may lash out at them because of his own grief. If he remarries, there is an adjustment to another woman in his life. In families where the mother had controlled the flow of information and decision-making between the father and the children, there is a new set of rules. Some women speak of getting to know their fathers better after their mothers died. When my husband and I married, it was my father who helped me plan my wedding reception.

As the roles shift, suddenly even small decisions take on monumental significance. Where should you hold Thanksgiving dinner? A sibling and his or her spouse who choose to spend Christmas alone after Mom dies may be perceived as abandoning the family. There are no easy and uniform solutions to these conflicts. But one way to keep them from escalating out of proportion is to understand that each of us deals with the loss of a mother differently. Just as our relationships with our mothers are personal and unique, so is the connection we seek after their deaths.

A daughter's path to reconnection with her deceased mother is an intensely personal journey, different from that undertaken by her sisters.

Some may seek reconnection sooner than others. One daughter may actively endeavor to understand her mother as a woman, while another may choose not to face her feelings. This is a personal journey, and we would do well to respect each other's pathway.

"After Mom died I went into her jewelry box and I took this bracelet of hers that I always borrowed," Barbara says. "At the funeral, my sister saw it and asked me what I was doing with it. I told her this was what I needed." Barbara was not stealing the bracelet. She was seeking what she needed: a physical reminder of her mother.

With our feelings and an open mind, we can begin to unravel this most complex of relationships as we seek to understand our mothers as women. That is the next step on the Path of Understanding, which we will undertake in chapter 3. But first we must look inside ourselves, examining honestly how we feel.

Connections

Despite all my best efforts to deny my feelings, it was not hard for me to get in touch with my emotions surrounding my mother's death and my relationship with her. All I had to do was stop running away and think. Then, from a perspective of loving myself and seeking a deeper connection with my mother, I could experience the sadness, anger, loneliness, resentment and all the rest. It began with honesty with myself, and ended with love for her and myself. For daughters whose mothers are still alive, it is imperative that they are completely honest with themselves about their feelings toward their mothers. Too often we are emotionally held hostage by anger, guilt and fear to explore our feelings. For example, to honestly admit that you felt abandoned at times by your mother does not condemn either one of you. Rather, it allows you to explore why you feel that way and to begin to understand the dynamics of your relationship with your mother.

From Feelings to Actions

- In a quiet moment, think about your relationship with your mother over the years. How well did you get along at the time she died? Did you have unresolved conflicts, or had your relationship matured as the two of you got older?

- Have you allowed yourself to grieve your mother's death? Have you bottled up the tears for fear of not being strong enough for your family?

- When you think about your mother's death, what is your gut-level emotion? Do you miss her? Are you angry with her?

- If these questions are frightening or too intense, consider seeking professional help in handling the emotions surrounding your mother's death. But for many women, these feelings are just below the surface of their lives, accessible to them if they only take a moment to contemplate.

I love stories—telling them, hearing them, collecting them. The reason, I believe, is that they contain powerful lessons in an easy-to-digest form. We all have our stories, memories that we recall and share. But when was the last time we unearthed a new story to tell ourselves? Tell yourself a story about you and your mother and later, if you wish, share it with someone close to you. Do not focus on the retelling to someone else, polishing the narrative for drama's sake. Relate it to yourself. See it play out like a movie in your mind. And let the story teach you, like all good stories do, about how you really feel inside.

Remember When . . .

- Remember the time you laughed the hardest with (or at) your mother. Did she have a saying that you and your siblings teased her about? Did she sing off-key or have any quirky habits? Was she funny? What would make her laugh? What did her laugh sound like?

- Remember the time you were the angriest at her. What was the injustice, real or perceived, that you vowed you would never forget? Did she belittle or criticize you at times? Was she too strict, or did she punish you unjustly?

- Remember the best present you ever received from her. Was it something she made or something she bought? Did she ever let you borrow something treasured of hers, like the one really good piece of jewelry that she owned?

- Remember a special one-on-one time with your mother. Were you home from school, eating chicken soup and crackers on a tray? Did you travel with your mother or go off shopping for a day? What was it like to be alone with her?

As you sort out your feelings, write them down. Putting the words on paper will shift the emotions from the internal to the external, creating a change that allows healing into your life. Be honest with what you feel. There is no reason for anyone else to read these pages unless you so choose. Do not censure yourself. You already know how you feel and you can't offend your mother anymore. Give yourself permission to feel your emotions without judgment.

The Mother Letter

- Write your mother a letter, telling her exactly how you feel. Write it out honestly and spontaneously. Don't rewrite it or copy it over, which may lead you to second-guess your emotions. Neatness doesn't count, and your handwriting need not be legible.
- Tear the letter into small pieces and put them in a non-flammable bowl. Light the paper and let it burn somewhere safely, either in an open window or outdoors.
- Watch the smoke drift up to the sky and know that the message has been sent.

The Daughter Letter

- Once you have written the Mother Letter, meditate for a moment on how you would expect her to respond. If you

believe she would be sad, angry or resentful, that probably reveals the feelings you harbor toward her and underscores the healing that is needed in your relationship
with her. But what if your mother, from a place of peace
and enlightenment, embraced your honesty and wanted
to heal her relationship with you?

- Write a letter to yourself as if your mother were speaking
  to you. Let your imagination wander. Hear in your mind
  what you believe she would say to you. Do not reread the
  letter before you finish. Let the words flow from you.

- When you are finished, read the letter once and then set
  it aside. Pick it up again in another quiet moment and
  see what the letter reveals to you.

3

Getting to Know Mother Again

*She wanted to devour the [scrapbook], to crawl
into it like a hungry child and take everything she wanted. . . .
Her hands all but shook at the sight of the cornucopia
that lay before her; clues to her mother's life, evidence
of her mother's life before children.*

—Rebecca Wells, *Divine Secrets of the Ya-Ya Sisterhood*

*W*ho was this woman who was your mother? You know her name, her birth date and when she died. You can probably recall her shoe size, favorite color and whether or not she colored her hair. She was your mother, your grandmother's daughter, your aunt's sister, and probably was your father's wife, at least for a while. She was the woman across the fence to the people next door; a friend to some and a nodding acquaintance to others. She was all these things and more.

Few of us really know our mothers outside of our roles as their daughters. And as important as the mother-child relationship is, it is not the only view of these women who came before us. They had entire lives outside of the context of the children they bore. They existed before we did and had lives after we left home. Our mothers did not belong only to us. Even if their lives seemed sheltered and insular, they belonged to themselves and to the world long before we came into the picture.

To understand our mothers as women, we have to step outside the tight, intimate circle of mother and child. We must reach out to others who knew her through a relationship that was different from ours. We must ask questions and listen with a curious mind and an open heart.

We do not seek anyone else's impressions as a way to cast away our own. Rather, each observation and every anecdote is like another brush stroke on a portrait. The face is already painted on the canvas, the features recalled from memory. Now there is the shading around the eyes, the blush on the cheek, the texture of the hair. Each detail brings richness and life to the portrait. As it is with paint and oils, so it is with a portrait of memory compiled from many, many sources.

In the Philippines, a special ceremony is held on November 1, the Feast of All Saints, in which everyone congregates in the cemetery to honor the dead. What makes this ritual special in my mind is that the prayers and tributes extend beyond each family's ancestors. Everyone gathers to honor all of the dead.

"We pray for our own dead and then we go to the next grave and then the next," explains Sister Mercedes Ventencilla, a nun who teaches in the Philippines.

Like holiday celebrants going from house to house, those visiting the cemetery stop at all the graves to honor the dead, from family members and distant relatives to friends and acquaintances. As they were known in life, they are honored in death. The dead are remembered in the collective memory.

We get to know our mothers through a variety of sources, seeking those who had different perspectives on who our mothers were as individuals.

So it is the same for us. We seek to get to know our mothers from a variety of perspectives. In some cases, particularly if our mothers died when we were very young, others knew her better than we did. In other cases, another person contributes a unique perspective on someone we thought we knew so well. Brought together, it is a powerful combination of collective memory.

On the Path of Understanding, as we get to know our mothers as women, there are three basic groups we seek to tap:

Our immediate family. While their memories and stories may be the same as ours, each individual has a different perspective within the family system.

Our mother's friends and peers, especially those who knew her before she married and had children.

Our own friends and peers who knew our mothers. This group may have the most unique perspective of all. They saw our mothers as women at the same time we experienced them as parents.

As we get to know the women who came before us, the portrait of our mothers will be enriched. Similarities with our own lives that we never saw before may suddenly be revealed. Or we may come to know a woman who is different from the image we had held. This process is not to shatter parental icons or challenge the views we hold about our mothers. Rather, we seek, from the perspective of adult women on our own journeys of self-discovery, to know our mothers more fully.

The Family as the Beginning

We start at the beginning, with our own families. For those of us with siblings, there is a ready source of information about our mothers, although it may seem redundant with what we already know. Regardless of the overlap, there is still value in talking to siblings about our mothers because each child has a unique perspective by virtue of birth order. An older sister remembers the day you were born. A younger brother recalls the day you left for college or got married. Just as each child in the family had a distinct relationship with his or her mother, their memories provide another view to share.

Chances are, if you have siblings, you have already discussed your mother. But now, listen to the stories with a different intent. Seek to understand how your siblings perceived and related to your mother. Even if their experiences are completely different from yours, they still reveal something of her life. Discussing memories brings out meaning that was not evident before, and also helps nurture bonds between siblings who may find fewer reasons to stay connected after their parents die.

From the perspective of understanding, even a light-hearted story becomes enlightening. Take the one my sisters and I tell about the Christmas our mother gave us identical dark green wraparound skirts and white blouses with smocked bodices, then got the same outfit for herself. It might have been cute if we had been under the age of ten, but I was a teenager and Jeannie and Bernadette were in their twenties. One day, two of us sisters and Mom ended up wearing the same outfit. Before the mad dash to change clothes, we looked like a strange adult Girl Scout troop.

Behind the humor, there is a deeper meaning. The story is an example of our mother's fairness. She never wanted to appear to favor one daughter over another. The problem, however, was that we sometimes felt she did not always see us as individuals.

Stories shared by siblings may help explain why our families functioned the way they did.

The stories shared by brothers and sisters can also unlock deep mysteries at the heart of our families. The intent is not to shame anyone or publicize family secrets. Rather, it may help to explain why our families functioned the way they did.

Jean Troy-Smith and her brother have combed over the details of their upbringing since their parents died. The process has brought the two of them closer and helped them reveal the secret that their parents had kept from them. Their father, Jean discovered after he had died, was an alcoholic. While he had stopped drinking, he never lost his abusive, alcoholic personality. Jean remembers her mother as a strong, positive force. But when their father said the children had to be punished, it was Jean's mother who doled it out.

"When my dad said we were to be punished and we were to be hit, she was the one who did it. She had to take his orders. She did not consider herself equal to him," explains Jean, an adjunct professor of English at the State University of New York at Oswego.

The discovery about her family led to understanding and ultimately to healing and peace. Jean's book, *Called to Healing: Reflections on the Power of Earth's Stories in Women's Lives*, is dedicated to her mother and father with the words, "Peace, at last."

"In death, they found the peace that they could not find in life," Jean says.

For some daughters, their fathers are a wealth of stories about their mothers' lives, revealing details about home life from a different perspective. "My dad will talk about Mom all the time," confides Betty U., a businesswoman in her fifties.

Talking to Dad also helps to nurture our relationship with him. For some women, the deaths of their mothers allows them to get to know their fathers in a new way.

"We always saw Dad in relation to Mom," explains Barbara, a professional in New York. "Now, we have a chance to get to know him as an individual."

Even if your father will not explain why your mother did certain things—he may well be of a generation that is still not comfortable discussing personal matters—seek out the stories he has to tell. It may be possible to glean an insight from a nuance or a casual comment.

Widening the Circle

As much as our immediate families know about our mothers, we cannot rely upon them as our sole source of information. We must look beyond them for a fuller understanding, reaching out to our mothers' peers and friends. We seek out those who knew her before we were born.

As adults, we know our mother's name is
not just "Mommy," but few of us have ever
contemplated our mother's identities.

It's hard to imagine our mothers as young girls, before diapers and orthodontist appointments, household budgets and home-cooked dinners. I'm reminded of the joke about the little child who, when asked what her mother's name is, replies very confidently, "Mommy." Certainly as adults we are aware that our mothers were not always mommies. But, on an emotional level, we may not have any sense of the women they were.

Other people knew our mothers well—when they were young, when they were single, when we were just babies in a stroller. Their memories add much depth to the portrait of our mothers.

We had a date, Aunt Jeanne and I, to drive to Mallory, New York, the small village where my mother grew up. I was back in northern New York with my son, Patrick, for a four-day visit with my father and my sisters. But the trip to Mallory was a mission I needed to accomplish.

"I don't know what you want to know," Aunt Jeanne, my mother's younger sister, said as she got into the car.

"Everything and anything," I replied, as we headed off.

Mallory is only a crossroads, but much had changed since 1924 when my mother was born. The sawmill is still there, but most of the big farms are gone. The forests have been cleared for new houses, while what was once open pasture has grown up into woodland. But as we cruised slowly along those country roads, my aunt's stories transported me back to the 1920s, where three sisters—Jeanette, Leona and Jeanne—walked to the one-room schoolhouse. In my mind I saw the farmhouse behind the three big maple trees and imagined the swing hanging from the upper boughs. I saw the pasture where Baum's bull got loose and chased a group of terrified girls to the front porch of their aunt's house. I saw my grandfather working the farm with a team of horses and my grandmother tending a garden that helped feed her family during the Depression.

I saw the little girl who would grow up to be my mother.

"Your mother was one of the bravest people I knew," Aunt Jeanne told me, launching into a story. "Papa had these huge work horses. Your Aunt Jeanette and I were afraid of them. But not your mother. She would stand in the pasture and call for them when it was time to put them in the barn. Those horses would come thundering down from the woods. Jeanette and I would run, we'd be so scared. But your mother would just stand there. She'd grab a hold of their bridles and lead them into the barn. When the horses moved their heads as they walked, they lifted her right off the ground."

My aunt told me story after story, including some I had heard from my own mother. But they were different, coming from my aunt. She spoke of my mother in the third person, revealing her own impressions of the young girl who would one day be the mother of three daughters.

I have a copy of a photo taken sometime in the 1920s. In it, Grandma holds Aunt Jeanne, who is a baby in a white dress. Aunt Jeanette, who looks to be no more than five years old, smiles into the camera. A younger sister, four perhaps, stands in front of her father, whom she resembles. Her eyes meet the camera lens and there is only a hint of a smile on her lips. I know that this little girl standing in the field dotted with daisies is my mother. But after hearing my aunt's stories, I have a sense of the child—loyal, stubborn and brave—that she was.

"Your mother loved you girls," Aunt Jeanette tells me on the telephone one Sunday afternoon. "Being a mother was the most important thing to her."

Our conversation has been filled with stories that I have heard so many times over the years—growing up in Mallory; dances at the USO during World War II; my mother's repeated collisions with the loading dock in Grandpa's big Packard. But Aunt Jeanette's voice softens when she recalls her sister's pride in being a mother. "The little dresses she made. The hats and gloves on Easter Sunday. She kept you girls beautifully."

"The first time I saw your mother, I was about fourteen and she must have been nineteen," recalls Aunt Margie. "I remember seeing her behind the counter at the bakery where she worked and thinking that this was a lady who knew where she was going."

Years later, Aunt Margie and my mother would be sisters-in-law. Aunt Margie married my father's brother, John, whom everyone called Fuddy, and over time my mother and Margie developed a friendship that went beyond their ties as in-laws.

As Aunt Margie talked, I could picture my mother as a young wife, some nine years before I was born. The two women, who were neighbors at the time, walked together nearly every day, pushing their baby strollers.

"We'd get all dressed up. It was our outing, you know. But we'd wear our flat shoes until we got as far as the lumber yard. Then we'd stop the strollers, take off our flat shoes and put on our high heels to walk through downtown," Aunt Margie laughed. "We couldn't possibly walk through downtown without our high heels on. Then we'd walk back home and, when we got to the lumber yard, put our flat shoes on again. Sometimes the guys at the lumber yard would be whistling at us."

I smile at the image. I can see my tall, slim mother, who always had great legs, changing her shoes on the sidewalk across the street from the lumber yard. I always had a sense of my mother as being a bit of a flirt, but in an innocent way. She was faithful and loyal to my father, but there was a hint of the coquette in her. It is a nice balance to the strict "church lady" that I also perceived as my mother.

The portrait of the woman who was my mother is developing. I see the girl in her face and the young wife and mother as well. I see the loyal friend and the woman with a wonderful sense of humor who was a natural storyteller. ("I remember when your mother was learning to cook," Aunt Margie laughed. "'I took that chicken,' she told us, 'and I stuffed it and stewed it and cooked it and baked it and it was still so tough you couldn't cut the gravy!'") I see the woman who was very private, with few confidantes, and who sometimes retreated when people got too close. Most importantly, I see the woman.

Janie's mother was an obstetrics nurse in Grant Hospital in downtown Chicago. Like Janie, a successful news media executive, her mother had a career before she married. On her Path of Understanding, Janie longed to know more about her mother as a young woman, single and living in Chicago before the days when she married and raised four daughters on a farm in central Illinois.

Janie wrote to her mother's old college roommate as well as to one of her aunts. Both women responded the day they received Janie's letters. They looked forward to sharing their memories with Janie and had already begun jotting down notes. The conversations Janie had with these women yielded some amusing anecdotes and several insights. From her aunt, she also heard stories about her grandparents, great-aunts and great-uncles, filling in the ancestral tapestry of her life.

"It's not only the information you might get about your mother, but also that of others in your family tree," Janie says of the interviews she conducted with her mother's friends and peers. "Even more important are the connections you make with those relatives who are alive and well."

Seeking out those who knew our mothers, we
gain not only insights, but a connection
with the previous generation.

Reaching out to others who knew our mothers, we deepen the connections of our own lives. A tie between aunt and niece is made more intimate. A woman who was our mother's best friend becomes more than just a familiar name. In asking our mothers' peers to share their memories with us, we also give them the gift of connection as they recall the woman they knew. Stories they had not thought of in years suddenly come back to them. They remember and see themselves with fresh eyes.

As we talk to our mothers' peers, we also establish ties to the generation of women who came before us. We have access to not only their memories but their perspective and wisdom as well. The stories they tell, the images they share and the anecdotes they relate are like pages of a history book, giving us context for our mothers' lives.

But there may be times when their stories do not appear to be particularly insightful. We may be secretly disappointed to hear a superficial account of who wore what when and went out with whom. Do not give up on the process. Give those you talk to permission to be candid with you. Ask what you really want to know. Share your perceptions of your mother and see if they concur. If you perceived your mother as a harsh critic, for example, ask your mother's friend or sibling. You may learn how critical she was of herself growing up. Or, as one friend told me, you may be pleasantly surprised to learn what your mother told others about you.

Mary's mother, like many women of the fifties, was sparing in her praise of her children. Many mothers of that day belonged to the school of thought that too many compliments would swell a child's head. So while Mary knew she was loved, she never heard much spontaneous praise. The day of her mother's funeral, however, she received an unexpected gift from a neighbor who had known Mary's family for years.

"She told me, in detail, how proud my mother was of me for things I had done and the way I handled certain things in my life," remembers Mary, herself the mother of three children. "I was so shocked. Mother had to have told her these things, because she knew the details."

These are the stories of our lives. What we learn about our mothers tells us as much about ourselves as it does about these women. The experiences our mothers had as children and young women shaped their opinions on everything from politics to religion to marriage to raising children. As their daughters, we were directly affected by our mothers' views of the world. Whether our mothers' lives embodied the proverbial good old days or our view of a personal hell, they are the backdrops of our own existence. These stories tell where we come from.

A Different Perspective

Our friends growing up got a glimpse of our mothers
as women, a perspective we long to discover.

Our friends came over to our houses, stayed for dinner and spent the night. For some close friends, our homes were merely an extension of theirs. Through this, our friends got a view of our parents and our families that offers an invaluable insight to us today. While we experienced our mothers as mothers, our friends got a glimpse of the women they were.

&

Like her siblings, Trisha was adopted. But in her mind the only mother she had was the woman who raised her. After the death of her father, Trisha's close relationship with her mother deepened into a friendship as the two of them took vacations together to Florida. Trisha, a psychotherapist, recalls those trips as "peaceful times" of enjoying her mother's company as a woman and a friend.

Not that they didn't have their conflicts, Trisha explains in her no-nonsense way. Her mother was tough and sassy as well as engaging and beautiful. "She had one wicked temper," Trisha says. "It was her strength and power."

But as close as Trisha was with her mother, there were still gaps in her knowledge about her parents and the wider circle of her family. She gained the insight when a cousin, Kathy, unexpectedly sent her a video she had put together from old home movies. In it, Trisha saw herself as a child from age two to eight, and her sister and brother as children. The scenes are random, but combined they piece together a nuclear family that was bonded in love.

"In the video, Mom and Dad are young and beautiful. There's my brother's First Communion. My sister and I are there in matching blue dresses. I'm goo-goo eyed as I look at my brother throwing a baseball. My sister takes my hand and we dance in a merry-go-round circle," Trisha recalls.

In another scene, the whole family clowns around in cowboy outfits; in another, Trisha's mother mouths the words, "Merry Christmas," to the camera.

"It was a gift beyond anything," Trisha says. She treasures not

only the video that enabled her to see the close and loving interactions among her parents and siblings, but also the connection it
forged with her cousin, Kathy, with whom she had not been particularly close in the past.

Since then, Trisha says she and Kathy have spent hours on the
phone, sharing insights and secrets of the extended-family dynamics, including the love and the anger.

❧

Michelle, a successful executive in New York City, has the good
fortune that she and her closest friends remember each other's
mothers during the years they were growing up. For these women,
there is a sorority of remembering.

"We say to each other, 'Wouldn't your mother have loved this?'
Or, 'What would she say about that!'" Michelle explains.

Her mother, whom Michelle describes as a "firebrand"—a practicing attorney in the 1940s who bristled at how "male" the estab-
lishment was—was a woman Michelle's friends looked up to. Her
mother encouraged not only her daughters but their friends to set
their sights on high goals. "She called people out to get on the road
to success," recalls Michelle.

Sometimes our search to learn more about our mothers
stems from a need to fill in the gaps in our own memories. It
may be that we were very young when our mothers died, or
that so much time has passed we are beginning to forget. Or,
as in the case of Barbara, we may have suppressed some memories along with our pain.

∂⁀〰

Some twenty years after her mother's death, Barbara S. found there were things about her mother that she could no longer remember clearly. Now, married and the mother of three, Barbara has sought to fill in the gaps of her memory by talking to those who knew her. Beyond her own siblings, she has sought out her cousins for whom her mother was a favorite aunt.

"They told me my mother had this knack of picking out just the right present. She was very thoughtful with gifts and picked out just what they wanted without knowing it ahead of time," Barbara recalls.

It is a quality that Barbara is pleased to find in herself. "I take a lot of time picking out gifts for people. I try to find something that I believe they will really want. I guess my mother and I have that in common."

How do our friends' perceptions of our mothers stack up with what we experienced?

Is there confirmation or a sharp contrast? Do we sometimes feel that our friends got to know the best parts of our mothers? Did our friends experience only our mothers' public personae, while we saw the "real" women underneath?

The answer, I believe, is that each perspective is part of the women who were our mothers. Beyond the confines and conflicts of the mother-daughter relationship, a complex woman emerges. There were more facets to her personality than we may have imagined. It may not all be beautiful or loving, or tortured or negative. Our mothers, like ourselves, are more than likely an emotional composite.

In her novel of mothers and daughters, *Divine Secrets of the Ya-Ya Sisterhood,* author Rebecca Wells looks at the sometimes painful complexities of this intimate relationship. "Mama taught me a lot of other lessons about femininity too. Some of them carry marks that no cosmetic can erase. . . . My mother slapped my cheek, where sometimes it still stings. My mother also laid her . . . soft palm on my girlish face and just cupped it there, for love."

I go back to my photo album and flip between two pages. One is a family picture taken in the fall of 1985, less than a year before Mother died, before anyone even suspected cancer was spreading through her body. The other is the little girl in the field of daisies. The two photos span some fifty-odd years, but there is a remarkable similarity between them. It is my mother's expression: a straight gaze into the camera and only a hint of a smile. The little girl and the grown woman emanate strength and composure, confidence but also a little distance. There are other photos where Mother appears more beautiful, and others were she is playful and laughing. But I am drawn back to these two, believing they reveal the core of her personality that never changed over the years.

Sometimes the photographs reveal a woman we hardly know, although her face is as familiar as our own reflection in the mirror. We see a picture from our mothers' pasts, literally a snapshot in time. The woman captured in the black-and-white, colored or sepia tones may be an intriguing mystery that we long to understand.

Gilda contemplated images of her mother, Gertrude, who was born in Russia in 1901, and moved with her family first to a Jewish community in Canada and later to the United States.

"I never knew the shy girl nuzzling flowers at her high school graduation, the grinning young woman in knickers posing with her friends at a YWHA [Young Women's Hebrew Association] camp, the twinkly woman who signed her engagement photo, 'Yours, Gertrude,'" Gilda writes. "By the time I met my mother, she was mostly serious; she seemed to look upon personal pleasures with disdain. I hardly remember a photograph of her smiling after she married. What happened to the shy girl, the grinning young woman, that twinkly woman?"

In Her Own Words

Even more revealing are the words our mothers left behind, in letters, diaries, poems and stories. Read years later, the writings are an echo from a distant time, at once historic and yet contemporary.

"I always knew about her writing. She was a professional journalist off and on in her own life and had toyed with fiction as well," filmmaker J Clements says of her mother, Ann Conger. "But I never knew about the depths of her journals. After she died we were cleaning out her things and there were all her journals. Some were leather-bound from her adolescence and some were spiral notebooks from the 1970s and some were loose pieces of paper she had written in the mental hospital."

J Clements's journey to understand her mother, who was a patient in a psychiatric hospital for a time in her life, resulted in her film, *Means of Grace,* which has been aired on PBS.

Reading the diaries, which provided wonderful insights and produced some painful revelations, J says she got to know her mother as a woman, a peer, outside the parent-child relationship.

"I feel like I know her almost as well as her closest girl-friend," J explains. "I've heard the words from her heart. It's as if she's been whispering in my ear."

Diaries, never intended to be a public document,
may reveal more about our mothers than
we are prepared to know.

Intensely personal and often not meant to be read by any-one other than ourselves, a diary holds a wealth of thoughts, dreams, troubles, aspirations and musings. It is an intimate portrait of someone's internal life and, when the writer is our mother, an unequaled chance to get to know her. But since a diary is usually not meant to be a public document, it carries the caveat of bearing some mixed blessings. Diaries may reveal more about our mothers than we were prepared to know.

"Take your time and do it slowly," J Clements advises daughters who may have access to their mothers' diaries. "Go with the understanding that she was another human being, not just a mother and a wife. Be prepared to see some things that will shock you. But you are going to feel closer to her."

Many of us may wish we had the gold mine of insight that a diary or journal offers. Unfortunately, so many of us do not. Lisa, a writer and journalist, stumbled upon her mother's attempt to write her memoirs and was disappointed that she never wrote more than a few pages. But that does not mean we are empty-handed. Even a letter tucked away in a drawer may reveal much about our mothers as they reflected upon their lives. Scrapbooks also give us clues to the women who kept them. What we treasure, after all, says much about our dreams and the way we live.

As far as I know, my mother never kept a diary. She had a scrapbook and kept a coat box full of mementos like the Christmas card Dad gave her when they were dating and birth announcements for us three daughters. What she also had, and I treasure now, was a small notebook that she wrote in during a trip to Europe that she and I made in the summer of 1976, between my junior and senior years of high school. Looking back, I only vaguely remember my mother writing in this notebook each evening during our trip, recording her memories. Rereading it now, I can see beyond the carefully recorded travelogue. "In the afternoon, we arrived in Baden. We stayed in a beautiful hotel with a moat around it. The flower gardens were just beautiful. . . ."

What this little journal shows is my mother's excitement on her first trip abroad, her enthusiasm for everything she saw and experienced, and a desire to know life beyond her day-to-day world. "As I walked down the street, I didn't believe my eyes. I couldn't believe such a wonderful thing was happening to me."

I cannot say that I had forgotten that about my mother, but it was good to be reminded of it. Ours was not a perfect relationship, if such a thing exists. Years after this trip, Mother and I would experience our share of bitter conflicts. A brief, disastrous marriage when I was twenty-three to a man who was abusive caused a rift between Mother and me that never completely healed. As I struggled with my independence, I found her to be a force that was nearly too big to fight against. When she was dying, I simply put those conflicts aside, knowing there was not much time to sort things out. I told her I loved her and she told me the same.

Understanding our mothers is a journey not unlike finding one's self. It is not a one-step process. Human beings, thankfully, are much too complex for that. Each discovery that answers one question may bring up ten more. Sometimes the lines between fact and perception are too blurred to distinguish.

I go back to the old composition notebook my mother wrote in during our trip through Austria and Switzerland. The pages, some of them loosened from the string that holds the notebook together, are tinted brown by age. I look at the loopy handwriting that is nearly as familiar as my own and realize that Mother has left me, most likely unconsciously, another clue about life. All we can do is experience it one moment at a time, and record what we see and learn along the way.

Connections

Each relationship in our lives reveals another facet of who we are. Your colleagues know you in one way, your friends in another. Your siblings experience you in one way, your spouse in another. As it is with us, so it was with our mothers. To understand who our mothers were as women, we look beyond their role as parents. We consider them as wives, daughters, sisters and friends by reaching out to others who knew them. This broadening of perspective offers insights into our mothers' personalities, whether they are alive or dead. Encourage the women you know whose mothers are still alive to try some of these exercises. Chances are they will learn things about their mothers that they never knew or fully understood before.

In the Family Circle

- Talk to your siblings about their memories of your mother. Compare observations and feelings, but do not try to convince anyone that your point of view is right or theirs is wrong. While your siblings may know the same stories you do, their unique perspective could reveal an insight into your mother.

- Talk to your father about your mother. Listen for nuances in understanding as he recounts the stories you may have heard dozens of times.

- Sharing stories about your mother with your family helps to maintain ties, particularly with siblings, that may weaken with the death of a parent.

In the Circle of Peers

- Contact your mother's contemporaries—her sisters and brothers, in-laws and friends—who knew her well. If possible, seek out those who knew her before she married and had children. Their stories may offer details of her life that help build a more complete portrait of your mother as a woman.

- Give your mother's peers permission to be candid with you. They may sugar-coat certain details of her personality out of respect for her and in an effort to spare your feelings. Tell them you want to get to know your mother honestly. Tell them your perceptions of your mother and see if they concur.

In the Circle of Friends

- Talk to your own friends and peers who knew your mother, particularly when you were growing up. Ask your friends what they noticed most about your mother, how they were treated by her, and for any personal memories they can share.

- Recall what it was like when your friends came to visit. Did your mother like your friends? Who was her favorite? Was there anyone she disliked? Ask yourself why.

A Mother's Thoughts

- Reread any cards or letters your mother sent you that you may have kept. Search your own scrapbook.

- If you have access to your mother's diary or personal papers, consider reading them for the insights they reveal.

- Examine your mother's scrapbook or memory box. What did she keep? What did she treasure? What do these things tell you about her?

Our relationships with others are not the only way we reveal ourselves. We show something of our personalities, our interests and the way we view the world through our taste in books and movies. Two people reading the same book, even decades apart, connect through the common experience.

A Favorite Book

- Read your mother's favorite book, even if it is not your taste. Ask yourself what it was about the plot, the setting or the characters that was so appealing to her. How does the story reflect her life, her goals, her unrealized dreams?
- Rent your mother's favorite movie. Try to see it through her eyes. Is there a character who reminds you of your mother or someone in her life?

A Face from the Past

- Study a photograph of your mother taken when she was young, preferably before she married and had children. What does the expression on her face tell you?
- Study her eyes and her smile and notice your own reactions. Is she vibrant or shy? Does she seem connected with the people and the setting around her, or does she seem uncomfortable in herself and her surroundings?

The women who came before us are waiting to be discovered. They are present to us not only in our own thoughts and recollections, but in the collective memory around us.

4

The Traumatic Relationship

Then a dark shape comes to occupy
that light, a figure in the shape of my mom with
a wild corona of hair and no face but a shadow. She has
lifted her arms and broadened her stance of her feet,
so her shadow turns from a long thin line into a giant X.
And swooping down from one hand is the
twelve-inch shine of a butcher knife. . . .

—MARY KARR, *THE LIARS' CLUB: A MEMOIR*

It is inconceivable that the woman who was supposed
to love and nurture you could do so much damage. But
that is the powerful paradox of the mother-daughter relationship. She who gave us life also had the ability to make us rue
the day we were born.

Exploring our relationships with our deceased mothers often
means dealing with traumatic memories. We may recall sharp,

wounding criticism or spankings that went too far. Or perhaps there were episodes when alcoholism or mental illness took our mothers away—emotionally or physically—and we were abandoned to our fears that somehow we were to blame. There may have been sexual abuse by a father, brother or another male relative that our mothers refused to acknowledge or prevent.

Scars remain, carved deeply in the soul.

Dealing with the traumatic memories is excruciating. For one thing, it is difficult to admit, even to ourselves, that our mothers weren't always good, kind and loving toward us. We make excuses in our own minds for our mothers' behavior, or else we question our perceptions. Compared with what some other people went through, we tell ourselves, it wasn't really all that bad.

The deeper motivation, I believe, is shame. We fear that by admitting our mothers did not always act lovingly toward us, we are stating that there is something fundamentally wrong with us. We fear being unlovable. If our own mothers couldn't love us, how could anyone else?

The fear of being unlovable plays out in countless ways in our lives, especially in our personal relationships. Daughters who perceive they were not loved adequately by their mothers or who felt they were rejected by their mothers are cruelly drawn to bad relationships. Or in our insatiable neediness, we can sabotage even a promising one.

"[Traumatized daughters] run around with an umbilical cord trying to attach to other people in unhealthy ways," says Dr. Joyce Fraser, a psychologist in St. Clair Shores, Michigan, who specializes in women's issues.

Healing Through Honesty

Healing of the traumatic relationship does not come from pretending that everything with our mothers was perfect, or from an attitude that it somehow didn't matter. On the Path of Understanding, we must examine our relationships with our mothers with honesty. If we gloss over the bitterness or refuse to acknowledge the conflict, we deny ourselves a piece of our own stories. All influences, including the negative ones, brought us to the point at which we are today. Moreover, getting to know our mothers as women, we must look at them as complete human beings with both frailties and strengths. Our mothers were not perfect any more than we are. In the most benign cases, they exercised poor judgment at times, stubbornly clung to outdated ideas and held back their support for our latest adventure for fear we might fail. In more traumatic situations, their anger and fear caused them to lash out at us, or else the pressures of the real world made them retreat from us.

Understanding the negative and traumatic elements of our relationships with our mothers does not excuse any abusive or harmful behavior. But it does give us an opportunity to acknowledge the pain that we may have spent a good part of our lives trying to avoid. It also allows us to free ourselves from destructive, addictive behaviors—such as alcoholism, drug abuse, excessive overeating and spending disorders—that are often a daughter's own rejection of herself. The first step is acceptance—admitting exactly what our relationships were with our mothers, with openness and honesty.

*As adults, we try to see the complete picture
to understand the reality of who
are mothers were.*

The Complete Picture

Even when the overall mother-daughter relationship was good, we must still acknowledge the bitter memories—not to put an undue emphasis on the negative, but to see the complete picture. As adults contemplating our emotional roots, we can handle the truth of who we are and who are mothers were.

"It is important for the daughter to understand the relationship with her mother and to seek and find answers to her questions regarding why the 'trauma' occurred, in order to put both of their lives in perspective," advises Dr. Michelle Iyamah, a psychologist with Iyamah Behavioral Healthcare, Ltd. of Chicago. "I believe that understanding—sometimes termed insight—is quite important to being able to recover and rebuild from a damaging mother-daughter relationship," she adds.

*It is impossible to have a "perfect" relationship
with anyone, including our mothers. The truth is,
we all have faults that become all too
apparent in close relationships.*

The fact is, it is impossible to have a "perfect" relationship with one's mother, or one's partner, friend, children or any human being. We all have faults that in the context of a close relationship manifest themselves. For us daughters, getting to know our mothers as women obliges us to see them as completely human—flaws and all.

Opening the Door to Healing

All too often, we daughters blame ourselves for the faulty relationships with our mothers. Believing ourselves to be responsible, we internalize the negative feelings surrounding the relationship. Learning why our mothers acted the way they did—even if their behavior was severely damaging—can heal us years later. Sometimes the understanding brings empathy for our mothers, knowing that they had acted out the pain they experienced in their own lives.

For some women, examining the negative elements of their relationships with their mothers is too big a task to handle alone. Even if the idea scares you or makes you feel vulnerable, don't abandon it and push ahead with some self-numbing activity or attitude. This does not erase the pain or break the chains of negativity that can bind all of us if we don't actively take the steps to free ourselves. With a little help, we can unearth what we've hidden away in the recesses of our minds, like the box of junk we push to the back of the storage closet to deal with another day. Now it's time to open that box, to sort through the junk and cast away what is no longer good, useful or safe to keep, and make room for the things in our lives we treasure.

To do that, we may seek help from a psychologist or other counselor. Or we may choose to deal with the negative memories on our own, perhaps reaching out to a trusted friend who can listen without judgment. If we need help, we allow ourselves to seek it. We no longer choose to let guilt or fear keep us from looking at the full picture of our mothers, ourselves and our lives.

The Traumatic Echo

For many women, negative memories of their mothers revolve around criticism that was relentless. Daughters felt devalued in their mothers' eyes, leaving them to wonder what they could ever do to win approval. Words became weapons that wounded deeply, and even decades later women deal with the traumatic echo. As grown women, they still perceive themselves as too big, too scrawny, too loud, too mousy, too slow, too stupid. Unconsciously, they gravitate toward people in their lives, especially men, who reinforce their negative self-image.

❧

Carolyn, a beautiful, vivacious woman in her fifties, recalls her mother's endless tirade of criticism that she was too big and clumsy, awkward and ugly. "I had no self-esteem left," Carolyn says. "None."

Intellectually, Carolyn saw the parallels between her mother's behavior and her own upbringing. Her mother, one of thirteen children, had been shipped off by her parents to the care of a wealthy aunt and uncle, who sent her off to a convent boarding school.

"As I was growing up, she would tell me how her aunt was mean to her, criticized how she looked, and bought her shoes that didn't fit because her feet were big," Carolyn recalls. "Then my mother would buy me ugly brown-tie oxfords, not pretty little Mary Janes, and tell me I had to wear them because my feet were so big."

Carolyn endured her mother's criticism through two marriages and the birth of her three children, until she could take no more. In the midst of a difficult divorce, Carolyn severed her ties with her mother. She could not handle her mother's criticism, Carolyn decided, and survive the breakup of her marriage. It was a painful choice, but at the time the only way she could survive emotionally.

Emotional Abandonment

For other women, the trauma lies in the emotional disappearance of their mothers. Alcoholism, depression or mental illness took their mothers away emotionally and sometimes physically. Intellectually, a daughter may know as an adult that her mother was battling internal demons that sapped her strength. But the child inside remembers the mother who withdrew, leaving her feeling emotionally bereft and abandoned.

Johanna remembers her mother pulling away from the family during bouts of depression, when even the simplest routines became too much to handle. "In the years when I was growing up, my mother was beaten down in her own head by depression," Johanna explains. "She loved me, I know she did. But if something wasn't convenient for her to do or if it wasn't easy, it wasn't done."

The eldest of four children, Johanna also bore the brunt of her mother's criticism. While she now understands that the criticism was a reflection of her mother's poor self-image, she still hears the hurtful words that left her own self-esteem in shreds.

Doris F. never experienced the nurturing mothering she craved. Her own mother, a Holocaust survivor, was too high-strung and emotionally damaged to connect with Doris or her sister. The mother that Doris experienced was a fearful, anxious woman, trapped in an unhappy marriage. While Doris is sympathetic to the horror that her mother experienced, she cannot forget or forgive the insidious verbal abuse that she and her sister suffered.

"She was a very damaged person," Doris says sadly.

Marks That Do Not Fade

Some women bear marks that do not fade. The angry red spot where a hand hit a child's soft flesh too hard, or the welt from a leather belt lashed across the legs is no longer visible. But the marks remain, nonetheless, on the daughter's self-esteem. I am not speaking about a slap on the wrist or a swat on the bottom. I am talking about the spanking that went too far, the punishment that became abusive, the punitive hit that became a beating.

While mothers may have lashed out in anger, frustration and pain caused by their own traumatic childhoods or abusive relationships with men, it was their daughters who received the blows. Physical abuse can never be allowed or excused. But the reasons for a mother's behavior can be explored and, in time, understood.

❧

Jessica remembers what it felt like to be hit with a hair brush or a fly swatter. The nearly forty years since her childhood have done nothing to erase those negative memories.

"She hit me, not often, but every once in a while. She just lashed out. She made me so fearful of her," she recalls.

As an adult, Jessica knows that her mother was angry and frustrated by an unhappy marriage. But as a child, she experienced her mother's anger directed at her for not obeying or being a "good girl."

"I just could not please her, even when I was a small child," Jessica says. "I have no good memories of her."

As an adult, the eldest of three children, Jessica received the sharpest criticism of all the siblings from her mother. Nothing she did seemed right, and when Jessica rebelled in her twenties by abandoning her mother's standard of beauty and attractiveness by cutting her hair and refusing to wear makeup, she was belittled and criticized. Her husband, Jessica's mother told her, would stop loving her and would abandon her unless she "kept herself up."

The eldest daughter, being her mother's first "experiment" in parenting a female child, often receives the biggest dose of her mother's criticism.

The eldest daughter in the family, it seems, receives the biggest dose of her mother's criticism. As the eldest daughter, she was her mother's first "experiment" in parenting a female child who reflected so much of herself. Insecurities surfaced as a mother relived her own childhood through her experience of motherhood.

In an era when feelings were seldom acknowledged and rarely discussed, our mothers may have acted out negative behavioral patterns from their own lives. Again, this does not excuse what our mothers did. But it does help to answer the persistent question of why they acted the way they did. More important, it also underscores the deep need for each of us to be healed at the core of our mother-daughter relationships. Without a deep understanding of who we are and who our mothers were, we may be doomed to committing the same mistakes in our lives and with our children.

The Tragic Death

For some of us, the trauma is death itself. Whether our mothers die long before we can conceive of them leaving us or they take their own lives, it is this sudden separation that causes the trauma that a daughter must deal with the rest of her life. Elizabeth was eight years old when her mother died. Now in her forties, Elizabeth feels she has little or no connection to her mother, who is now only a shadowy memory. Emelia's mother committed suicide, throwing herself in front of a train to escape the pain, depression and despair brought on by an alcoholic marriage and the onset of breast cancer.

The day her mother killed herself, Emelia recalls, the police had been called to the family's apartment because of another fight between her parents, brought on by a bout of drinking. Enraged and embarrassed, Emelia confronted her mother and left the apartment to spend the night with her aunt and uncle.

"The following morning, I went back with my aunt and uncle. My father was still in a drunken stupor. My mother wasn't at the house," Emelia recalls. "We all got in the car to look for her. I thought, My mother is dead. And sure enough, she had killed herself. She jumped in front of a train."

That was fifty-seven years ago, when Emelia was fifteen and her mother thirty-seven.

When the Relationship Dies

For some women, even though their mothers are still alive, the relationship between them is dead. Severe conflicts, physical or psychological abuse, or wounding criticism sever the link between mother and daughter. The relationship is dead, and a daughter mourns the loss of what she did not have with her mother.

"There are some horrible relationships between a child and a mother," says Reverend Janet Campbell. "The healing can only happen with separation."

But there is still an opportunity for redemption and healing that comes, Reverend Campbell believes, "from accepting the reality."

❧

Bright and professionally successful, Sarah's outward life belied the traumas she had endured. As a child, she had been sexually abused by her uncle, grandfather and a family friend. As an adult, she was married to a man who abused her emotionally, verbally and sexually. In therapy, Sarah sought to examine the events of her life and her feelings. That led to an exploration of her relationship with her mother, who was also an incest survivor.

Her mother had never acknowledged that Sarah was sexually abused, nor did she try to prevent it. An emotionally immature and needy person, she later used Sarah to solve her problems, including relying on her for money. The only way Sarah could survive this emotional manipulation was to separate herself from her mother's sickness. Since her mother refused any counseling or therapy, Sarah's recourse was to place strict limits on their interaction, including using an answering machine to screen her calls.

"There is no magic cure for extremely disturbed relation-ships between mother and daughter," advises Dr. Iyamah, who shared the story of Sarah (not her real name), a composite case study from her work with survivors of sexual abuse.

"Sometimes it is necessary for the daughter to completely separate from the mother, in order to heal and develop an independent sense of self. Sarah and her mother will likely never have a relationship in which her mother is nurturing, supportive and appropriate in her interactions. Sarah has come to accept this reality."

Acceptance does not mean we excuse what happened to us. Rather, we admit to ourselves what we experienced. "It comes from realizing that everything you experienced was true. You were not validated. You were not loved. It was all true," Dr. Fraser adds. "Then you shift the perspective. You understand who your mother was and what she was dealing with. Then you know that what you experienced *was not about you*. Your mother did not reject you; she rejected herself."

The Silent Rage

Remembering the traumatic episodes may unearth a host of uncomfortable emotions—rage, resentment, remorse. Our fear of these emotions, which may lurk at the edge of our lives, has kept us from delving too deeply into our own pasts. Instead, we have tried to skirt that boulder inside ourselves, sometimes brushing up against it, but most of the time staying as far away as we can. You know the boulder I mean. The stone that blocks that secret place inside yourself, that cave where we store all our unspoken anger and unvented rage. But that stone and that cave are taking up an awful lot of room inside ourselves, space that could be freed up for other things—like self-love, creativity and nurturing relationships. To make room, we have to roll away the boulder and let the light of understanding and the air of truth into the cave.

What comes out of that cave may be anger so old that it is expressed in a child's terms. "I hate you, I hate you, I hate you." Or it may have no words at all. It may be a cry or scream of pain.

Whatever it sounds like, let it out. We have been stuffing the pain and anger into that cave all our lives and shutting it fast with the boulder of denial. Fear has prevented us, until this point, from opening the cave. But we are no longer afraid that these negative emotions will be more than we can handle. There is nothing in that cave we didn't put there ourselves. Every hurt, every slight, every unmet need. Every criticism that cut to the core. We know the inventory of our caves even without exploring them.

In a quiet, safe place, preferably when we are alone in our own homes, we can allow the feelings to surface. Anger. Sadness. Resentment. We feel the emotions rising out of the hidden caves inside us. Giving voice to the emotion as it rises, we allow the cry, the moan or the wail. We *express* the emotion—in both meanings of the verb; we put our feelings into a word or sound and we send it out.

❦

"I yell at my mother sometimes," admits Johanna. "I don't do this in the middle of my office, but if I'm alone in my car, I'll yell out loud at her. I'll ask her why she acted the way she did. Why did she miss the boat so badly?"

Venting that anger and frustration has helped Johanna move beyond the pain and into a place of understanding. Depression, Johanna sees clearly, was an enemy her mother could not fight. Expressing her anger and pain also has helped Johanna separate herself from the negative aspects of her mother. Although she considers herself to be hypersensitive and prone to depression as her mother was, Johanna says she fights it head on. Remembering how her mother retreated from the family during bouts of depression, Johanna makes a conscious effort to be involved in the lives of her two children. Knowing how it felt to be criticized, she tries to build self-esteem in her children.

"I do feel at peace with her," Johanna says. "She did the best that she could, given her own limitations. I did not come with a set of instructions: more hugs now, more pats now. She didn't read any instruction manuals."

Balancing the Positive and the Negative

Expressing our emotions creates an emotional shift in our lives. No longer held prisoner by our fears or blocked by our traumatic memories, we are free as adults to take stock of our relationships with our mothers. For many women, that means acknowledging both the positive and negative aspects of our relationships with our mothers. If we deny that there were any conflicts, we repress part of ourselves. Conversely, if we dwell only on the negative, we ignore any nurturing or love we received.

One way to take stock is to literally make a list. In one column write down the positive elements—the fact she cared for you when you were sick, went to all the parent-teacher conferences, bought you presents for birthdays and holidays, helped care for your babies when they were born, etc. In the other column, write down the negative ones—the sharp criticism that tore down your self-esteem, the emotional distance that left you craving love and physical affection, the standards that were too high to achieve and that made you feel as if you were doomed to fail.

Examine the list. Take in the positive aspects. They are still part of the relationship even if they seem to be outweighed by the negative elements. The mother who spoon-fed you chicken soup when you had the measles still existed, even though she criticized you for being too loud and clumsy. Take an honest look at the negative aspects. Did her criticism reflect the way she herself was treated as a child? Were the too-high standards that she set an extension of the way she was raised? Was she emotionally distant because she was sapped by family, health or other pressures?

Understanding the traumas is the first step toward healing. Through understanding, we gain some emotional space from the traumas that haunt us.

Understanding the traumas from our childhoods goes a long way to healing them. When we take a step back, looking at our mothers from the perspective of adult daughters and not as wounded children, we can see more clearly. By understanding how and why our families functioned the way they did, we can separate ourselves from the traumas and negative behaviors that occurred. We can also take our share of the responsibility. We may have lashed out at our mothers as much as they lashed out at us. Acknowledging this, we forgive ourselves and move on.

Choosing to Heal

Acknowledging that a relationship was traumatic at times does not condemn us to be victims. Rather, it is the first step in setting ourselves free. Healing, like much in life, is a choice we make by putting ourselves first. We seek professional help from a supportive therapist in dealing with severe traumas and abuse. We bravely look inward to acknowledge and understand the negative memories that mar an otherwise positive relationship with our mothers. In each case, it begins with the decision to look at our own lives, unravel the self-defeating patterns and put our needs first.

This is such a difficult concept for so many of us, as we were raised with the notion that to make our needs a priority is to be selfish. Everything and everyone else must come first, we believe. We put ourselves in last place like cheerful martyrs, then bitterly resent the hell out of everyone. We watched our mothers do the same thing, then lash out at us out of anger and frustration. If nothing else prompts us to seek healing, it should be this realization: Unless we break the chains of negativity, we will add our link and pass it on to our children.

"You try to seek as much help as you can; you need to get support from wherever you can get it—friends, a psychotherapist," says Doris F., who went through twelve years of psychotherapy to deal with the trauma of her childhood. "For me it was a long road to recovery. It still is."

By taking charge of our lives and responsibility for ourselves, we look at the parenting we received not to cast blame, but to understand. Where damage was done, we look for healing. By ourselves or with a therapist, we begin a process of "reparenting," counteracting the negative patterns and behaviors that affected our young lives. We become healthier and our self-esteem is rebuilt. Most important, we stop sabotaging ourselves and tearing ourselves down.

Silencing the Negative Voices

One way to heal is to stop that critical voice in our minds, the one that sounds like an angry, berating parent. "You are so stupid," we say to ourselves. "You can't do anything right." "You look like shit today."

But we cannot quiet that voice in our heads—the one that seems driven to tear down whatever self-esteem we have left—until we understand where it comes from. Like an echo in a canyon, the self-destructive words we hear in our minds did not originate in the present moment. They are reverberations from another source, bouncing off the walls of our subconscious minds. The source of that self-criticism is our own past.

I remember being nineteen and carrying twenty extra pounds, which on my five-foot-one frame looked like twice that amount of weight. I knew my tall, slim mother was concerned about my weight, though she did not say so overtly. Then she told me a "story" that, in retrospect, was probably well intentioned, but at the time cut me to my core.

"This woman I know, whose name I'm not going to mention, stopped me in the grocery store today," I remember Mother telling me. "She said to me, 'How could you let your daughter get so fat? She used to be so thin.'"

I instantly doubted that there was "some woman" who told that story to my mother. I believed she was telling me how disappointed she was that I was overweight. I read in that story her disapproval—not only of the fact that I was twenty pounds overweight, but of me, period.

The truth is, I needed to lose weight, and in time I managed to do just that. But I have had an uneasy relationship with my own body all my life, being an anorexic 94-pound high school senior, and then weighing well over 135 pounds a few years later. It is a pattern in my life that I am well aware of, knowing that too much of my self-esteem comes from an unhealthy fear of being fat. The five extra pounds that creep onto my body on occasion can spark a lot of self-loathing. A diet and rigorous exercise will take off the five pounds. But only love will take away the negative images.

Like many women, I have a love-hate relationship with food, my solace and my punishment. When I'm feeling tired, stressed or overloaded, comfort looks like a toasted bagel. When I'm really tired, stressed or overloaded, comfort looks like two bagels. While the carbohydrates give me a boost, it sets off a self-deprecating chain reaction. "Why did you eat that?" my critical voice asks me. "You are going to get fat."

That is the self-esteem demon I wrestle with as I try to take a healthy approach to my body with a good diet and exercise, like running. But I can cover one hundred miles in my jogging shoes and get nowhere if I do not approach myself and my mother with love.

Breaking the Chain

Berating ourselves serves no good purpose. It does not build character or make us humble. True humility, after all, is a knowledge of who and what we are. Regardless of whatever unique gifts each of us have, we are all alive, healing and yearning for more. That is a powerful place to start.

We replace cruel self-criticism with affirming statements. Using the first person, "I," we give ourselves the words of love and encouragement we long to hear. Our internal dialogue changes from the damning words of "You really screwed that one up" to a nurturing one: "I did the best I could" or "I made an error in judgment. Next time I'll try a different approach."

> *To experience self-love, we should treat*
> *ourselves like our own best friends.*

The only way to exorcise the internal demons is to tell them to leave. No more biting self-criticism. No more making fun of yourself—even if you think you're making a joke. Think about the Golden Rule of loving your neighbor as yourself, and reflect upon the inverse. Love yourself as your neighbor. We should treat ourselves the way we treat our best friends. Loving ourselves, we allow ourselves to heal. Healing, we are strong enough to consider reconciliation.

Seeking Reconciliation

Sometimes reconciliation with our mothers comes only after they have died. While our temptation may be to dismiss it as "too late to do any good," it is essential to recognize that this negativity still dwells within us. Understanding our mothers and, if we choose, reconciling with them after the trauma we experienced frees us from the chains of negativity. We may, on a spiritual level, believe we seek reconciliation with our mothers for their sakes. But the truth is, we do this for ourselves and the generations that will follow us.

Carolyn maintained a distance from her mother and, by extension, from her father for several years. When first her father became ill and then her mother was diagnosed with cancer, Carolyn decided to reconcile with her parents, but on her own terms. While Carolyn needed to stay away from her mother during her divorce from her second husband, who was an abusive alcoholic, she eventually found the emotional resources to approach her again.

"My mother asked me why I had stayed away for so long," Carolyn recalls. "I told her, 'because you criticized me so much.' She nodded and said, 'I understand.' That was it. She never mentioned it again."

Her mother, perhaps painfully aware of her own mortality, never criticized Carolyn again. By the time her mother died, she and Carolyn had reconciled. Although she struggles with her self-esteem, Carolyn has overcome the negativity. "I don't let anything get me down," she smiles. To know Carolyn and to be around her, one can appreciate how far she has come.

The Forgiveness Conundrum

Forgiveness is a tricky concept. For many of us, forgiveness was something we had to do in order to be good girls. "Forgive us our trespasses as we forgive those. . . ." We remember the phrase from the Lord's Prayer, but when it comes to our own lives, the words may stick in our throats. We don't want to forgive. Forgiveness means that what was done to us didn't matter. It means it was okay that we were abused and traumatized. It means that we were never hurt, physically, emotionally or psychologically.

Wrong.

Forgiveness—acceptance or reconciliation, if we prefer those terms—means choosing to move on. It means understanding. But it never means we condone what happened to us.

On the Path of Understanding, we must remind ourselves that it is never okay for us to be abused or belittled. It is not loving or in any way beneficial to have our self-esteem shredded by hurtful criticism, or our souls withered by a lack of love and praise. But by coming to terms with our relationships with our mothers—understanding that their negative behaviors were often a reflection of how they themselves were raised, or a by-product of the traumas of their own lives—we may feel empathy for these women. We may even wish we could have helped to heal them while they were alive, releasing our mothers from the pain of their lives.

Whether or not a daughter can bring herself to reconcile with her mother is a completely personal choice. Understanding why the traumatic or abusive behavior occurred may be all a daughter chooses to do. Empathy may be as far as she will go.

"I cannot forgive her. Maybe that's wrong, but that's just the way it is," says Jessica.

The only peace Jessica experiences now in relation to her mother is knowing that, in death, her mother can no longer perpetuate the criticism that tore at Jessica's center.

"She was a good woman, a good person, I can see that," Jessica explains. "But she was a lousy mother."

Knowing that her mother was acting out of pain in her own life helps Jessica to understand why her mother acted the way she did. But that is as far as Jessica can go.

Dr. Fraser, herself the daughter of an emotionally unavailable, alcoholic mother, suggests that forgiveness need not be part of the process at all. Rather, through acceptance and understanding of what occurred in their lives and the lives of their mothers, daughters can undergo transformation.

"It is not in my power to forgive," Dr. Fraser says gently. "It's in God's power to forgive. For me, I am going to find my power to heal. That's the moment of transformation."

Lessons and Blessings

The transformation stems from a shift in perspective, from being a victim who blames everyone else for her troubles to being a self-empowered adult. It also means looking at the positives and negatives of one's life and seeing what treasures can be recovered from the rubble.

For Emelia, life has been a mix of lessons and blessings. Many of the lessons came out of tragedy—her mother's suicide; the untimely death of her first husband, who was the love of her life; a divorce from her second husband.

"I have been truly blessed, I will say that," says Emelia, now seventy-two, who runs weekend retreats for those who are grieving the loss of a relationship due to death or divorce. "I have been blessed with joys, sorrows and happiness. Without the firing in the furnace, the steel does not become strong."

Her mother, Emelia has come to understand, was in a deep depression long before she took her life. Through that understanding, a connection remains between mother and daughter that is born of the love that existed in their relationship, a tie that could not be broken by death.

"I remember sitting on my mother's lap when I was fifteen. I was physically touched and loved by her," Emelia recalls. "My own kids have always sat on my lap. I've cuddled them because that's what I learned at my mother's knee—hugs and kisses."

What Emelia remembers now is love that extends beyond the grave.

The Imperfect Rose

None of us has a perfect life. We experience trials and tragedies as well as the victories. We are imperfect, as are those around us. Still, we can manage to be magnificent and triumphant. This message was brought home to me one summer morning.

In my garden that morning was a very imperfect rose. As the bud was forming, a rabbit took a bite out of one side, nibbling away the first few layers of petals before the blossom opened. But the rose continued to form and later bloomed. On this particular morning, three-quarters of the rose was perfect, unfolding layers of coral-pink petals like ruffles on a petticoat. But one-quarter of the rose was missing, with only the ragged edges to remind me of the damage wrought by a rabbit. A few days later, the rose had bloomed fully, opening its petals to reveal its golden center. Fully mature, the damaged petals were completely compensated for by the unfolding of the blossom.

There may have been some damage caused when we were children, but we still managed to bloom.

We are all like that rose. There may have been some damage caused when we were children, most likely unintentionally, as our mothers reacted to the stresses of their own lives and upbringing. But we still managed to bloom.

By understanding our mothers, our family systems and ourselves, we can break the chains of negativity. We can acknowledge the pain experienced by the child inside us, but choose to move to a place of healing.

We invite love into our lives—from our friends, our partners, our family members with whom we are close and, most of all, from ourselves. On a spiritual level, this love that surrounds us flows from a never-ending Source, which we may call God, our Higher Power or the Universe.

"God makes available to us in our lives what is lacking and what is needed," Reverend Campbell states. As we unearth, examine and heal the traumas of our lives, we need to bring this love into our lives. It may feel like the firm grasp of a lover's hand in ours, the soft skin of our child's cheek against ours, the warm sunshine on our faces in the garden, the soothing music we play in a quiet moment, or the hush of a church, temple or meditative place. Regardless of what has occurred in our lives before, we are just as we should be. Even if we have ten things on our wish list of getting better—from eating more fiber to taking up in-line skating—we are fine just the way we are. Accepting ourselves in the moment, we can move on into tomorrow. All the chastisement and self-loathing in the world won't bring us an inch of improvement. It will only recall the sorrow that emanates from a dark, secret place inside.

Roll back the boulder and unblock the cave. Put an end to our emotional death by choosing life and health. How? By choosing, understanding and seeking love—the most important being self-love.

A Difficult Lesson

Most of us give lip service to self-love. We know that without loving ourselves, it is impossible to experience anyone's love for us. We know that unless we take care of ourselves, we cannot take care of anyone else. We know all this. Putting it into practice is another matter.

The problem, I believe, is that self-love does not come naturally to adults. For children, it is another matter. Watching my son grow and develop, it was easy to see he had no problem asking for his needs to be met. As an infant, he wailed loudly when he was hungry or wet, or needed to be held. He communicated his needs, and to the best of our abilities my husband and I met them. But in time my son, like all of us, began to learn that he was not the center of the universe. He had to wait in line, share his toys and understand that he could not have everything he saw. He became "socialized," as the term goes, learning to live in society and to get along with others.

But for many of us, the need to adapt and in some cases subjugate our needs to the good of the whole went too far. We made the transition from the innate selfishness of young children to selflessness, but then we continued on the road to self-negation. Somehow we came to believe that our needs did not matter any more. Traumatic experiences from our childhoods reinforced our warped perceptions that we were unlovable and undeserving. We stopped asking for what we truly wanted and needed, slipping into a perpetual state of resentment over everything that everyone else had (or so we perceived). Not believing in our own self-worth, we devalued ourselves.

When the anger and frustration built to a critical mass, we lashed out in a frenzy of what we thought was getting our needs met. It usually involved a binge of some sort or a damaging relationship that, in the end, only reinforced our lack of self-esteem. We booby-trapped the system against ourselves. We set ourselves up to fail. We chose people who could not love or value us. We didn't love ourselves enough to make better choices.

Like many women, there have been times in my life when my only experience of self-love was the noticeable absence of it in my life. And in all truthfulness, I must admit that this is a concept I wrestle with still. The negative experiences of my childhood, from feeling I did not measure up in my mother's eyes to being the target of taunts and mean-spirited jokes in school, reinforced a negative belief that I did not count. A brief, disastrous marriage to an abusive man when I was twenty-three bore out my complete lack of self-love.

Now I know that self-love is the only way to move forward. It is the only cure for the wounds of the soul, the only escape route from the negative patterns of the past. The more severe the trauma, the more urgent the need. But how, I have asked myself, can I develop this self-love, which only I can give myself?

Self-love can be a cup of coffee savored slowly in the midst of a hectic rush. It can be a hot bath while the kids are busy with a computer game or a video. Self-love can be saying no, not now, to a pile of laundry when the flower garden, an old friend on the telephone or a pair of jogging shoes beckons. Self-love can also be saying no to the bridal shower for a third cousin's daughter-in-law-to-be because the house is a complete wreck. It is whatever seems kindest and most loving to ourselves at the moment.

Self-love will mean different things at different times of our lives. What is loving for one may not be for another. A week at a spa may be a self-loving gesture for some of us, allowing into our lives nurturing and pampering that we have forsaken for too long. For others of us, the thought of being away from home for a week or of spending that much money when we're struggling with credit card debt may seem like hell rather than paradise. Maybe sitting with our feet up on the sofa while listening to music we like to hear, unplugging the phone and ignoring the housework, is the best medicine.

Self-love does not mean shirking the responsibilities of our lives, which for many of us women include jobs, homes, families, children, pets. But it does mean that we can and must put ourselves first at least part of the time. The house will not crumble if we take a well-deserved rest. The family will not starve if we allow someone else to cook for a change. We will not become lazy and slothful if we spend an hour flipping through the pages of a catalog, with no intentions of buying anything, rather than tackling the next chore.

For me, self-love is a fifteen-minute hot bath while reading a paperback. No matter what else I have to do in the evening, I allow myself that bath, a brief but important reminder that in a busy family with two working parents and an active child, my needs count, too.

Making Up for the Hurts

As we move into a place of deeper self-love, we draw into our lives gentleness and nurturing. We cannot erase the trauma and pain of our pasts, nor can we explain the great disparity between mothers who loved their daughters deeply and purely and those who inflicted damage. But we can open ourselves to the redemptive power of healing, allowing love and understanding to take the place of anger, bitterness and self-loathing. We invite love and healing into our lives, which can come at any time and any age. It does not depend on having a lover, spouse, children or even close friends. It does not require money, worldly success or fame. All we need is to look at the woman in the mirror, acknowledge the journey she has traveled thus far and give her permission to be.

Connections

For most of us, our relationship with our mothers is a mixture of the bitter and the sweet, the negative and the positive. Acknowledging this reality is the first step toward healing the traumatic mother-daughter issues that linger in our lives. Even if we consider our relationships with our mothers to be, on the whole, positive, we cannot pretend the negative aspects did not exist. This is not to place too much emphasis on the negative, but simply to see our mothers—and ourselves—as complex, multidimensional human beings. This honest examination of our relationships with our mothers can be done at any time, regardless of whether our mothers are alive or deceased. If your mother is still alive or if you share this book with a friend who is struggling with her relationship with her mother, this exercise can help sort out the positive and negative aspects.

Making a List

- Divide a sheet of paper into two columns. Label the right column "Positive" and the left one "Negative." Now write down, honestly, the positive and negative aspects of your relationship with your mother. Did she care for you when you were sick? Did she always remember your birthday? Write those things in the "Positive" column. Was she overly critical? Did she play favorites among her children? Put these items in the "Negative" column. Don't rush through this exercise. Be specific and write down as many elements of your relationship as possible. The list can be compiled over several days.

- Be honest with yourself. No one—not your spouse or your siblings—has to see your list. It is not for publication or posting on the kitchen door. Don't edit your list as you go along. If your first thought is that your mother criticized you too much, don't retract the thought later because "she was trying to build your character." The list is not to assign blame, but to understand the feelings and issues that linger.

- When the list is complete, honestly examine it. What is the overall tone of the list? Do the positives outweigh the negatives, or the other way around? Taking stock of the elements of the mother-daughter relationship will help you understand her better when we examine the historical, cultural and other influences on her life, as we will in chapter 5.

Many of us learned over the years to suppress or deny our feelings of anger, rage, hurt and resentment, stuffing them in a cave deep within ourselves. We shut that cave with a boulder, the one that feels like a knot in our stomachs or a weight on our chests. It is time to roll away the boulder and unblock the cave. Once emptied, the cave can fill with love, nurturing and the things in our lives that we cherish. When someone first suggested that I had to get in touch with my hidden anger, I was nervous at the prospect. I was afraid of breaking down, losing control or simply feeling all that rage. So I put it off. Then one day I got mad, I mean really pissed off, and I started to vent. It all came out—the hurt, resentment, fear, anger and rage that I had held back for years. When it was over, I felt completely spent. But there was a lightness to me that I had not experienced in years.

Unblocking the Cave

- In a safe, secure place (preferably when you are alone in your own home), allow yourself to feel the hurt, anger, sorrow, rage and whatever else is deep inside you. These are the same emotions you've felt before, but like most of us, you tried to put a lid on them. This time as the feelings emerge, don't block them. If you feel like crying, cry. If you feel like yelling, yell. If you feel like screaming, scream. (That's why it's best to do this exercise when you're alone and not with your children, who could be frightened or confused by your outbursts.)

- In a quiet, soothing atmosphere, feel your body and mind being bathed and replenished by healing, white light. Enhance the experience with quiet music, the sounds of nature or the reverent hush of a worship place.

Like many women, I'm usually doing two things at once. I talk on the phone while I clean the bathroom or cook dinner. I read or edit while I ride the train to work. I do one thing while I think of another. It is a phenomenon that Faith Popcorn, who tracks and predicts consumer trends, calls 99 Lives. "The modern motto of 'Too Fast a Pace, Too Little Time' . . . forces us all to assume multiple roles in order to cope with busy, high-tech lives," Faith wrote in *Clicking: 16 Trends to Future Fit Your Life, Your Work, and Your Business*. The problem is, all this rushing around to accomplish everything that needs to be done leaves very little time for taking care of ourselves. But without that nurturing, we cannot possibly replenish our reserves, leaving us unable, in time, to take care of anyone—including ourselves. What we need is a healthy dose of self-love.

Loving Ourselves

Think of the gifts you can give yourself as a token of self-love. They do not have to require any money, and if finances are a problem, it would *not* be loving to ourselves to compound the situation with a frivolous purchase. If your budget allows for an extra treat, large or small, think about what you truly desire. Here are some random examples:

- Pet the cat. Scratch the dog's ears. Hug the kids. Hold a hand. Touch is very healing for all involved.
- Listen to music. Rent a video, even if you're the only one in the house who will watch it.
- Browse the stacks in the library. If you never took the time to get a library card, do so now. Check out the classic you always wanted to read, the adventure novel that whets your appetite or the romance that transports you away. Read about the life of someone you admire.
- Sit with your feet up for at least fifteen minutes. Let the answering machine take the calls; the laundry and housework can wait.
- Take a half-hour walk on your lunch break. Have lunch with a friend, even if you both brown-bag it at the company cafeteria.
- Have a manicure, pedicure or facial, or give yourself a bit of pampering at home with a soak in the tub.
- Laugh, out loud, a lot. Smile.

5

Influences in Our Mothers' Lives

We are born at a given moment;
in a given place; and like vintage years of wines,
we have the qualities of the year and of
the season in which we are born.

—C. G. JUNG

Imagine you are on a long, transcontinental flight from New York to Paris. You cannot sleep and the in-flight movie is boring. Thankfully, the person sitting next to you wants to chat. You begin to talk about yourself, sharing one story and then another. Your fellow passenger listens intently, asking questions and telling a story in return. One story follows another until you have revealed much about yourself and your life. You have told your life story.

We all have them, these chronicles of our lives, from the curriculum vitae of our age, profession, education, marital status and whether or not we have children. But there are other stories, ones that reveal more about our upbringing, our views on life, our vital experiences, our tragedies and our triumphs. When we share these stories, we allow another person to get to know us. We reveal the clues of who we are, deep inside.

Understanding our mothers as women, we contemplate their life stories. Most of us heard our mothers' accounts of their younger years, how and when they met our fathers, what it was like the day we were born. Or perhaps our mothers were no longer alive or were not emotionally available to us, and so the stories came from other sources. Most of us know, at least, the basic facts.

Searching for a clear picture of who our mothers were as women, we go back to the stories, even if we've heard them countless times. We go beyond the simple facts and details that ceased to be interesting because of our overexposure to them. We look at the stories anew for the nuance and revelation. Like a detective combing for clues, we seek the threads and themes that ran through our mothers' lives.

In a novel, movie or play, the historic time frame and the physical settings are key to the development of the characters. As it is in art, so it is in life. We cannot fully understand our mothers without comprehending the context of their lives. Were our mothers born into affluence and privilege, or was it a daily struggle to survive? Were they wrapped in a cocoon of conformity or did they buck the system? Did they stand as equals to the men in their lives or walk ten paces behind them? What ethnic and cultural influences played out in their lives? Did they experience prejudice or turn a blind eye to it?

As we look to understand these women who came before us, we choose to step out of our own lives and into theirs. We go back in time intellectually to understand what influenced them in their early years, before we were born. What so-called "truths" did they encounter from their mothers before them; what did they reject and what did they accept?

Our mothers came of age sometime during the twentieth century, an era of incredible change. In this century, we have gone from gaining the right to vote to sitting on the Supreme Court. We gained civil rights and fought for equal rights. We became clerks and secretaries, taking over what had been male occupations in the last century, and rose to the ranks of corporate officers and chief executives. We shortened our skirts and lengthened our responsibilities. We bobbed our hair, and then let it down as we experienced social, economic and sexual freedom. Whether or not our mothers were at the forefront of change or clung to the old ways, they were part of the evolution.

Our Mothers as Daughters

As we begin to understand our mothers as *women*, we quickly come across the one area in which we have common ground. Our mothers were also daughters. As simple as it may seem, we often forget that the woman who raised us was raised by another, who was raised by another, and so on back through time. Just as we were influenced by our mothers, so they were shaped by theirs. No matter if we are following closely in our mothers' footsteps or on a completely different path, our journeys began in the same place—with our mothers as guide and example.

Whatever our mothers taught us about love, truth, sex, God, femininity and the role of women helped form our consciousness—whether we agree or dismiss every word of it. Just as our mothers' attitudes became the basis of the lessons they passed on to us, many of these same views are what we pass on to our children.

Understanding the context of our mothers'
lives offers us the key to who they were as women.
Their attitudes about men, marriage, sex and success,
which they passed on to us daughters, were
shaped by their own life experiences.

Some of these attitudes are truly family treasures, which should be preserved and passed down as a legacy. I'm speaking of values such as loyalty, honesty, compassion, social conscience and nurturing love. But some attitudes are the burr that causes the callus on our souls. We became irritated, wounded and scarred by attitudes and so-called "truths" that we rebelled against but could not quite cast off. The only way to heal is with understanding.

The "Mother Myths" and the Secrets to Life

Interviewing women for this book, I came across a few of what I call Mother Myths, bits of fact and fiction that were passed down to us as the laws of living. Sadly, many of these "truths" were delivered in the form of an admonishment, prefaced by the words "you had better" or "you had better not." Yet on a deeper level, I believe these admonishments were really what our mothers saw as the "secrets to life," which they sought to pass down to us *from the perspective of their own lives.* What we may have taken as criticism may have actually been advice that was well-intentioned, even if sharp-edged in its delivery. Here are a few of the common Mother Myths that, when explored, offer insight into the way many of our mothers experienced life.

"Why Buy the Cow . . . ?"

"You had better not sleep with a man before you're married, or at least not before he gives you a ring!" Many daughters, particularly the Baby Boomers, were chastised into chastity by our mothers' view of premarital sex. Remember the old saying, "Why buy the cow when you can get the milk for free?" For those of us who did not adhere to our mother's rule of sexual abstinence, the admonishment felt more like condemnation.

What was behind this apparently prudish behavior? Consider the fact that, after World War II, there were more marriage-aged women than men. With this kind of competition for a husband, preferably a "good provider," a woman's virtue took on even more importance as a prize. After The Pill and the sexual revolution, social mores changed, and virginity until marriage was no longer the accepted norm. But the romantic modus operandi of the 1950s called for an alluring woman who engaged in a little heavy petting with her steady boyfriend or fiancé to show she wasn't frigid, yet who remained a virgin until she married. The warning against premarital sex, therefore, may have been a protective Mother Myth to keep a daughter from throwing away her chance of being a "good catch" and condemning herself to being a second choice or, God forbid, an "old maid."

The Virtue of Typing

"I don't care what you think you want to do, you had better learn to type!" How many women actors, dancers, physicists, physicians, research scientists and other professionals faced that admonishment? The ability to type, which I must say has served me well in my years as a journalist and writer, was promoted as a virtue by many of our mothers. We may have interpreted this advice as a sign of our mothers' lack of confidence in our dreams, talents and ambitions. But I believe the virtue of typing was promoted for an entirely different reason.

Consider the scant employment opportunities that were available to our mothers. Women executives were rare, and virtually no one outside the pages of the movie magazines made a living as an artist. And women who lived through the Depression knew that being employable was as important as a seat on the life raft when the ship was sinking. Did our mothers seek to kill our dreams of becoming a tennis player or a dancer, or did they fear for our ability to take care of ourselves should the bottom fall out of everything?

"Don't Count Your Chickens . . ."

"Expect nothing and you won't be disappointed" was one of my mother's favorite pieces of advice. Having gone through the Depression and her share of disappointments in life, my mother, who could be funny, upbeat and charming, had learned to keep a lid on her expectations. Built-up hopes, she believed, made her vulnerable for a fall. There are many variations on the "don't count your chickens before they hatch" theme. Sometimes there are cultural superstitions that reinforce this belief. Some Italians believe you can attract the *malocchio*—the evil eye or jinx—by boasting, bragging or even accepting a compliment. In Yiddish, a boast or even a hopeful statement could trigger a *kenahurra*, the setup for a fall. Life was simply more precarious for the generations before us, who may have experienced the horrors of the pogroms, the hardship of the Depression or the angst of the polio epidemic. Tempting fate with optimism, in their view, was a foolish way to live.

A variation of the same theme is the "you may think you have it bad, but somebody has it worse" attitude. One friend shared her mother's favorite saying: "Think of all those women whose husbands never came back from World War II" was her mother's answer to every disappointment her daughters experienced. Today, with New Age beliefs and metaphysics moving toward mainstream, many of us believe we get what we create, attract what we think, and have to visualize before we can achieve. But for the generations before us, that attitude would have been feared as an invitation to disaster.

To unlock the Mother Myths and the secrets to life,
we look to the forces that shaped the lives of
the women who came before us.

Each of us has her own set of Mother Myths and secrets to life, passed down to us from the preceding generations. To understand them, we have to look at the forces that shaped the lives of our mothers. Surely, personality and personal circumstances played important roles in their lives. But the historic, cultural and societal backdrop are also key. To unlock their views of themselves and the world, we look to what they experienced firsthand.

We journey back in time intellectually, seeking to view the world as our mothers did. Each of our mothers had her own story and unique life experience. The ones that follow are only a few examples of the themes that ran through their lives.

Suffragettes, Flappers and Eleanor Roosevelt

The 1920s roared with change. Having won the right to vote, thanks to the untiring efforts of suffragettes, women of the 1920s got a taste of equality with men. But activism did not end there. "For a long time, historians thought that feminism ended in 1919, at the moment that women got the vote," explains Catherine Lavender, a professor of history at the College of Staten Island, City University of New York. "But women continued to be active."

That activism, Professor Lavender adds, ranged from championing the rights of the poor to campaigns to end military conflict after the first World War. Women like suffragette and social activist Jane Addams took up the cause of the poor, the underprivileged and the newly immigrated.

Change in the 1920s also took place on a more superficial level, as flappers with their bobbed hair and short skirts danced the Charleston all over the social mores of their Gibson Girl mothers. Women smoked, drove cars and emulated the looks of the film stars in the silent pictures.

❧

"My mother bobbed her hair when long hair was the thing," Emelia, seventy-two, says of her mother, Lucia, who was born in

1903. "When she was young, she was so beautiful, she was asked to model. She danced with Rudolph Valentino when he came to Chicago."

Although the daughter of Italian immigrants in a very strict household, Lucia's beauty and love of arts and music broadened her world. "She was, in her time and in the old Italian neighborhood, the person everybody loved and looked up to," Emelia recalls.

The crash of the stock market and the dark days of the Depression changed the world. Money and jobs, or the lack thereof, became paramount, and women shouldered the burden of survival along with the men. Women of this time were often portrayed as the silent strength of the family, keeping together hearth and home, learning to make do and to eke out meals for the family with a resourcefulness that bordered on alchemy.

"It was thought that women were more able than men to endure the hardship. This put a kind of cultural pressure on women," Professor Lavender explains.

Women of the 1930s who sought a role model of self-reliance and strength had to look no farther than First Lady Eleanor Roosevelt.

The role model for many women in the 1930s was former First Lady Eleanor Roosevelt. Her husband held the reins of power, but it was Eleanor who ventured out into the world when Franklin could not. It was she who went into the institutions and down into the mines for the sake of her country and her husband.

As Pulitzer Prize-winning author and historian Doris Kearns Goodwin writes in the opening pages of *No Ordinary Time— Franklin & Eleanor Roosevelt: The Home Front in World War II*, "Franklin called Eleanor his 'will o' the wisp' wife. But it was Franklin who had encouraged her to become his 'eyes and ears,' to gather the grass-roots knowledge he needed to understand the people he governed. Unable to travel easily on his own because of his paralysis, he had started by teaching Eleanor how to inspect state institutions in 1929, during his first term as governor [of New York]."

As women ventured out into the world, they saw the ways in which they could make a difference. But in these early decades of social activism and reform, women's roles were often thwarted by the demands of domesticity.

᠅

Cynthia's mother was raised to be a socialite. Away from the Iowa farm where she grew up, she was introduced to the refinements of music, French lessons and dance recitals when she was a teenager in Oklahoma City. But during her college years in Boston, Cynthia's mother embarked on a different path, one that would give her a sense of purpose and responsibility, the echo of which would ring empty in later years.

"In her second year of college, she started touring orphanages and prisons, social welfare hospitals and settlement houses," says Cynthia, who learned much of the details of her mother's life from diaries her mother had kept.

After receiving a master's degree in social work from Radcliffe College, Cynthia's mother worked at a women's reformatory, where her responsibilities included the day-care center for young children whose mothers were imprisoned. Later, Cynthia's mother and father met and were secretly wed for fear he would lose his position at a Boston hospital that forbade medical residents to marry. Then Cynthia's mother became pregnant with her first child, quickly followed by three others, until she had four children under the age of five. Like many other women, family responsibilities forced Cynthia's mother to surrender the career that had given her a sense of self-worth and identity. Cynthia's father, meanwhile, practiced medicine, gaining recognition for caring for the wounded soldiers who returned to the United States during World War II.

"My mother had this terrible sense of feeling trapped," Cynthia says. "I grew up feeling that there was nothing worse than being a woman. Your fate was drawn for you. You were going to get stuck no matter what."

This theme would surface for many women in the later decades, especially in the 1950s when our mothers, who enjoyed economic freedom on the home front during World War II, gave it all up for domesticity.

Surviving and Thriving During World War II

*For immigrant women, change was profound
and permanent as they left the familiar for the new
and foreign. Many came with little or no money and
unable to speak the language, facing hardship,
separation and, sometimes, prejudice.*

Many of our mothers and grandmothers were among the millions of immigrants who came to the United States, leaving the familiar for the new and foreign. Change was profound and permanent, as many came without knowing the language or the culture, with little money and few skills except for the most vital one—the desire to survive. They left a culture and an identity that, in the days before easy and affordable transcontinental travel, soon became a slender tie to a different world. Leaving one country for another cleaved them from the familiar, even when they tried to re-create it by settling into an ethnic neighborhood in a large U.S. city.

Angela's roots are Italian, reflected by her lyrical accent when she speaks. A mother and grandmother and now seventy-two, Angela tells the story of her mother that is at once unique and at the same time illustrative of the hardships and triumphs of many families that immigrated to the United States. Her mother, Nicoletta, was born at the turn of the century in a small Italian city and married early in the 1920s. Nicoletta stayed behind in Italy when her husband left for the United States to find work. Returning in 1931, Nicoletta's husband stayed two years, during which time a second child, Angela's brother, was born. When her husband came back to the U.S. in 1933, that began a fourteen-year separation, during which time there was little communication and no visitation; only hope that Nicoletta kept alive during World War II, when Italy was part of the Axis and an enemy of the United States.

From 1940 until 1945, Angela recalls, there were no letters from her father because communication between the U.S. and Italy was not allowed. "We were concerned, but we knew he was working in this country and there was no war over in the U.S.," Angela explains.

With her husband gone, Nicoletta helped feed her family—and many of the neighbors as well—from her little farm and the garden she kept. She also enjoyed a special status in her town as the provider of wisdom and advice. Although society dictated that she had to be accompanied by a male relative to retrieve a long-awaited letter from her husband that was facilitated by the Red Cross, Nicoletta was clearly the power center and matriarch of the family. After World War II, Angela's father began the process of bringing his family to the United States. They arrived in March of 1947, after eleven days on board ship. After a long separation, it was little wonder that family became central to Nicoletta's life, as it is to Angela's today. Even though it meant leaving her native country behind and losing her status as a matriarch of the town, after the long and painful separation, Nicoletta wanted nothing more than for her family to be together again.

A Mother's Fear, a Daughter's Anguish

Sometimes our mothers' stories seem too painful to contemplate. But understanding what our mothers endured, from events that were beyond their control to poor life choices they made, helps us to understand them as women. And in that understanding, empathy is born.

Doris F.'s mother rarely talked about her childhood in a small town in Poland, or the horrors she experienced as a young Jewish girl in Dachau, from which she managed to escape. Her mother's younger sister, who had been the favorite of her parents, was raped and killed in the concentration camp. When the day came for Doris's mother to be lined up at the edge of a trench dug by the prisoners and shot, she somehow managed to escape the bullets. She pretended to be dead until the guards left the scene, climbed out of the trench filled with bodies, and ran into the forest.

Doris's mother was taken in by a farm family who hid her and later her cousin in the root cellar. "She had a lot of determination and a strong will," Doris says of her mother. "But she was very damaged. She never got over it."

After the war, Doris's mother and her cousin left Poland for a repatriation camp in Germany. It was there that her cousin fell in love with a man; Doris's mother decided to marry the man's brother, even though she did not love him. It was a disastrous choice for Doris's mother, who suffered through an unhappy marriage until her death.

Her mother's tragic life left her emotionally damaged and unable to give Doris the kind of mothering she needed. But understanding her mother's story has helped Doris to heal the damage she suffered and to go on with her own life.

"I did get some good parts from her—the resilience, the determination, the will to make something better for myself," Doris says.

Rosie the Riveter Rolls Up Her Sleeves

World War II also helped produce another kind of strong, self-actualized woman. We've all seen her image: Rosie the Riveter, her hair tied back in a scarf, displays her biceps as a symbol for the can-do spirit of the women during the war years. In the name of patriotism, women went to work, enjoying economic freedom in the 1940s—although for many this would be a short-lived experience.

"The dominant image in the forties is Rosie the Riveter," observes Theresa Kaminski, a professor of history at the University of Wisconsin–Stevens Point. "A lot of women moved into the factories, but also into other occupations as well. It was a time of women dominating higher education as they became teachers as well as students. Most of the colleges and universities kept going during the war years because women were enrolling."

The 1940s were also a time of freedom of another sort, as some young women saw it as their patriotic duty to have a brief, romantic fling with the servicemen. "It was the old, 'I'm being shipped out in the morning and there's a war going on . . . ,'" Professor Kaminski explains.

This "live for now" attitude during the war years also made for some hasty marriages and a rise in birth rates. But when couples were reunited as soldiers returned from the war, many realized the bad match they had made in haste. For the first time in history, Professor Kaminski explains, divorce was on the rise.

The end of World War II changed women's lives,
as pink slips were doled out to those who had
flocked to the factories during the war.

The end of the war in the mid-1940s also brought another profound change to women's lives, the shock waves of which were felt through the 1950s and into the 1960s. Women in the factories were given pink slips as war production was winding down and soldiers returning from the war needed the jobs. Rosie put down her tools and put on an apron . . . but the 1950s would not be the scene of pastoral domesticity that many tried to portray.

June Cleaver, or Not!

With the fifties came a widespread desire for stability, and many women heeded the call to domesticity. "On one hand it was a good thing, since families and making babies are certainly good," explains Brett Harvey, author of *The Fifties: A Woman's Oral History.* "But there were other elements that were not quite so benign. Motherhood and family were emphasized to the exclusion of everything and anything else."

Images of the fifties mother abound. And there are legions of us Baby Boomer daughters who were raised by women of the fifties, many of whom put home and family above everything else—especially themselves. Looking at the lives of the women of the fifties, we cannot avoid delving into the issues of domesticity, marriage, sex and careers. For many of us who continue to struggle with these same issues, a closer look at the fifties is enlightening.

In the 1950s, the term "housewife" was not the pejorative it is today. In fact, it was ironically descriptive. Many women of the 1950s appeared to be married to their houses, which were immaculate and obsessively cleaned. Daughters of the women of this era often recall that their mothers were not particularly demonstrative in their affection. They showed their love of their families through their service to them—from spoon-feeding chicken soup to sick children to an endless cycle of washing and ironing.

"There was a lot of propaganda urging women toward the June Cleaver role," says Katherine Jellison, a professor of history at Ohio University.

*Propaganda in the fifties urged women to
embrace the ideal of domesticity. Magazine ads from
that era show smiling, overdressed women gleefully
tending to the new, labor-saving devices in their
immaculate kitchens of the future.*

Thumbing through magazines from that time illustrates the point. Page after page shows overdressed women gleefully toiling in kitchens equipped with labor-saving devices—symbols of 1950s prosperity. A full-page advertisement in the April 2, 1956, issue of *Life* magazine, for example, shows a woman in a dress, high heels, hat and white gloves returning from the grocery store to fill her Philco Super Marketer refrigerator. In another ad, a smiling woman in a pink dress and high heels loads her new General Electric dishwasher. The April 1956 issue of *Ladies' Home Journal* includes an ad for GE's Roll-Easy Vacuum Cleaner, featuring a woman dusting draperies, carpets and bookshelves while wearing—you guessed it—a dress and heels. On another page, a brunette in an off-the-shoulder polka-dot blouse, slim-cut skirt and red high heels shows off her Gibson electric range that "lets you broil both sides at once!"

But there was another face to the 1950s. Some women, many with college degrees or careers they left behind, lost touch with themselves and their dreams in the domestic conformity of the time. Depression, mental illness, alcoholism and broken marriages were far more common in the 1950s than the smiling women in the advertisements would indicate.

❧

Amy, an entrepreneur in her forties, recalls the beautiful, charm-ing, alcoholic society wife who was her mother, the woman who was so consumed by her failed marriage that she could not nurture her daughter. Retreating to her country-club world of the late 1950s and 1960s, Amy's mother sought solace from friends and a drink. That left Amy to seek love and validation from the only other source in her life—her father, a very successful and charis-matic businessman. Unfortunately, that set up a triangle, to which many of us "daddy's girls" can relate: Unwittingly we became our mothers' rivals for our fathers' attention.

"She loved me, but she was threatened by me," Amy says.

A mother of two children, Amy experiences some flashbacks now to her childhood as she sees her daughter vie for attention from her own father. The family circumstances are different: Amy is married to a loving, devoted man who is nothing like her father, who later divorced Amy's mother and married a woman with whom he had been having an affair. ("My husband is so steady," Amy says appreciatively. "There is no way he would leave me.")

But the family dynamics that Amy is experiencing with her own daughter are eerily revealing. Her daughter complains about what she perceives as Amy's inattention due to a thriving business. It is the same complaint Amy harbored against her mother, only for dif-ferent reasons.

In a curious way, it has helped Amy feel an affinity with her mother, with whom she had a reconciliation of sorts before she died. A recovering alcoholic at the time, her mother came to care for Amy for a week when Amy's daughter was born. Two weeks later, her mother was dead due to an aneurysm. But she left behind in the freezer a legacy of the 1950s mother—countless meals, frozen and carefully labeled.

Sex and the Girl Who Wants to Marry

For the women of the 1950s, the pressure to be the perfect American wife meant more than just a shiny kitchen floor and a homemade, four-course meal. It meant getting and keeping a husband, which was both an art form and a strategic plan.

At the center was sex—a conundrum for many women of the 1950s, some of whom, author Brett Harvey discovered in her research, married just to have sex.

For many young women in the 1950s, their virginity was the ultimate poker chip in the game of romance and marriage. In the back seats of Buicks or a secluded hideaway where petting got more than heavy, the entire responsibility for how many bases were covered rested solely on the woman. "The standard was different for the girls of the fifties than [for] the boys. If something 'happened' it was her fault. There was no question," explains Brett.

Her mother, Debra realizes now, made a fatal mistake. She chose a man who attracted her sexually, but married out of her religious faith and her social class. Debra is convinced her mother's failed marriage, which she endured because her religion and Eastern European ethnic background did not allow for an annulment once children were conceived, was the cause of—or at least the main contributor to—her mother's mental illness.

"Although she might not have wanted marriage for many reasons, her romantic nature required it of her," explains Debra, a writer and historian in her forties who is married for a second time. "She had to marry because it was expected in her time and place in history. All her friends were slowly leaving the single, working life of the post-war era to have their 'boomer' babies, and their little picket-fenced cottages. It was expected of them all, reinforced by books, movies and songs. A woman of my mother's era could only be valued by the acceptance of a man with a commitment to marriage."

From the start, the couple realized they were ill-suited to marriage. They began the marriage cessation process, but a few weeks later, Debra's mother became pregnant. She was trapped, and a mental breakdown followed.

"In another time, another place, they each might have walked away to begin their lives anew. But when she failed the expectations of her ethnic society, she literally came apart in what was then termed a mental illness," Debra explains. "I think her 'troubles' began when she could not live up to what she viewed as a life plan."

Vanguards of Change

While many white, middle-class women were living—or struggling—with the rigidity and conformity of the 1950s, their African-American female contemporaries were living different lives. "The roles for black women in the 1950s were more like what women in the 1990s have experienced. They were working. They were involved," Professor Jellison explains.

❧

Lawanna, now thirty-four, remembers her mother as a strong, independent woman with an indomitable spirit. A divorced mother, Hannah, moved the family from Mississippi—where Lawanna was among the first to attend the newly desegregated schools—to Chicago. To support her family, Hannah worked as a seamstress and later as a manager at a retail department store. She went to school to learn to make fur coats, but never realized that dream when she lost her eyesight due to complications from diabetes. Still, Hannah never complained and remained self-sufficient and independent, drawing strength from her deep religious faith. She studiously learned Braille and took care of herself.

The Sixties and the Seeds of Change

The Civil Rights Movement. The Women's Movement. The Pill. Woodstock.

The images of the 1960s are powerful and lingering. But the sweeping changes did not begin with the stroke of midnight on January 1, 1960. For many, a restlessness and a sense of dissatisfaction with their lives in the 1950s was the spark that ignited a roaring blaze of change in the 1960s.

"If I am right, the problem that has no name stirring in the minds of so many American women today is not a matter of loss of femininity or too much education, or the demands of domesticity," Betty Friedan, a pioneer of the women's liberation movement, wrote in *The Feminine Mystique*, first published in 1963. "We can no longer ignore that voice within women that says: 'I want something more than my husband and my children and my home. . . .'"

Some women of the 1960s got jobs, studied languages or threw themselves into a flurry of household activities. Others embraced motherhood with a fervor, seeing it as a way to define themselves. Still others embraced the changes of the 1960s and joined the front ranks in the battle for change. They broke away from convention and shattered stereotypes in their own lives and in society.

❧

Mirah recalls her mother as an independent, free-spirited woman whose political and social convictions played out in her own life. Her parents met at a program for preschool teachers, where her mother had gone to help underprivileged children and her father was serving as a conscientious objector to the Vietnam War. Her mother, white and Jewish, and her father, African-American, married. Mirah sees this as part of her mother's statement about her personal and political beliefs.

"She was going to marry the man she loved and have a child with him no matter what color he was," Mirah says.

Even after her parents' divorce, Mirah's mother continued to teach her daughter about equality, identity and nonconformity. "She had a militant spirit," recalls Mirah. "She taught me not to stand for the National Anthem. She trained me to say 'I'm brown and proud' when I was four or five years old. By having me, that was the biggest political statement of her life."

Looking at the details of our mothers' lives, complex and often fascinating women appear. We begin to grasp the dreams that they chased and the ones that were unfulfilled, the heartbreaks of their young lives and the compromises of their later years. Our mothers emerge from their stories as women of flesh, blood and emotion. In that instant, we no longer stand as daughters looking up—or down—at our mothers. We are shoulder to shoulder with them, our peers.

"In order to know yourself and respect yourself, you have to know your history," Professor Jellison adds. "There is a lot of power in that . . . to see what women in the past have survived, what they have conquered. You can read about Eleanor Roosevelt or some impressive public figure, but it's a lot more meaningful for women to see the courage, the successes of people they really know."

Understanding our mothers as women, we gain an appreciation for their life experiences, both the good and the bad. We see how they were shaped not only by the times in which they lived, but also the culture and traditions of their families. We unlock the Mother Myths and secrets to life that they passed on to us as gospel, grasping perhaps for the first time where these so-called truths originated. We can disarm what looked like hurtful criticism and sharp admonishment. We distance ourselves from our mothers only to gain a better vantage point to observe their lives. Then we draw nearer with empathy, understanding and love.

We begin with their life stories, tales as familiar as our own, which we listen to in our minds one more time. We talk and we share stories that reveal an intimate portrait of where we came from, whom we were born to.

Draw nearer and listen. Sit inside the circle, close by the fire of warmth and friendship. Tell me your story, and I'll tell you mine.

Connections

We all have our stories that define us, tales of our triumphs and terrors, heartbreaks and healing. Our stories are like the proverbial onion skin, each revealing a little more as we peel down to the core of our being. The outer or superficial stories are for acquaintances or those with whom we do not have a personal relationship. The middle layer of stories, more revealing of ourselves, we share with closer friends and family members who know some—but not all—about us. The inner layer of stories are known only to our intimates. Then there is the core, the deepest level of stories that are known only to one, perhaps two, other people. Or perhaps we've never shared these stories; we're barely aware of them ourselves. In a composite, it is the book of our life.

So, too, our mothers had their stories about their day-to-day lives, dreams, struggles, marriages, children, illnesses, false hopes, miracles, losses and recoveries. Some of the stories we know well from hearing them so many times. But while we know the narrative, I wonder how many of us contemplated the meaning. What revelations in these stories have been available to us for years that we never considered before? If our mothers are deceased, we may look to our relatives to tell us these stories, or perhaps we can replay them from memory. For women whose mothers are still alive, ask to hear the stories once again, and listen as if you were hearing it all for the first time.

Storytelling Time

- Think about the story of your mother's life. Do you know the details of where she was born, what her parents did for a living, where she went to school, how she met your father?

- Write down the stories in a notebook as you remember them. They are a treasure for yourself, your siblings and the generations that follow. If writing does not come naturally, record the stories orally, using a tape recorder. Then go back and read or listen to the stories you have compiled. What nuance or meaning can you glean from them? What insight do they contain that you never grasped before now?

- Recount some of the most revealing or illustrative stories to a close friend. In return, invite your friend to reveal stories about her mother. What themes and insights occur to your friend that you have not considered?

- Share the stories with a sibling or an older child. Recount not only the story, but also the understanding. Share your insights and your interpretations. Help another to see and understand the woman who was your mother.

The Mother Myths: we've all encountered them—the advice we received from our mothers over the years in regard to men, sex, marriage, jobs, children and life in general. For many of us, these myths were often delivered in the form of unwanted commentary on our life choices or sermons on how we should be living our lives. But on closer examination, these myths reveal how our mothers viewed themselves and the world around them.

Mother Myths and Secrets to Life

- What advice did your mother dole out the most? What did she advise or admonish her children (particularly her daughters) to do or not do? Looking at the theme of her advice—whether it be about marriage, children or career—what does it reveal about how she viewed the world? Mothers who grew up during the Depression may have been expressing their own fears about financial security when they urged their daughters to pursue a practical career instead of an artistic pursuit. One mother's discouragement of her daughter's college career reflected what the mother herself had experienced growing up in a culture that did not value the education of women.

- What did she criticize most about you? Your appearance, your friends, your job, your husband? Set the pain and anger of the criticism aside for a moment. What had she hoped to gain with that criticism or unwanted advice? Were the critical comments about appearance (a common preoccupation among women of the 1950s) really a mother's attempt to help her daughter "win" or "keep" a husband?

- What did your mother say at the major events of your life? What did she say when you graduated from college, got married, changed jobs or had a baby? What wisdom did she share? What old wives' tale did she recite?

- What was your mother's favorite expression? Did she dole out caution about not "counting your chickens before they hatched," a common theme for those whose mothers saw danger in setting themselves up for a disappointment? My mother advised us to "expect nothing and you won't be disappointed," a complex little nugget that promised to ward off false hopes. It was also a jinx. But writing this now, I recall another of her expressions. "It costs nothing to dream," she'd say, which, while not a wholehearted endorsement for our plans, at least acknowledged the inherent pleasure of having dreams in the first place.

We may be among the first generation born in the United States or part of a long line of Mayflower descendants. In either case, our cultural and ethnic background influences our lives, as we embrace certain traditions or shun others. As we begin to understand our mothers as women, we seek to discover what cultural and ethnic influences existed in their lives. Did they consider women equal to men or inferior to them? Did our mothers act like a partner to our fathers or their servants? Were their religious faiths a source of strength or a controlling force? Did our mothers celebrate traditions from their culture or ethnic backgrounds, or try to hide or obliterate them? Did our mothers grow up in a society that viewed women as little more than decorative objects or as vessels to bear children?

Culture and Tradition

- Consider your mother's ethnic and cultural background. What does it explain about her behavior and attitude? How did she view herself and other women—particularly her daughters—in light of her own upbringing?

- How much do you know and understand about the ethnic and cultural backgrounds of both your mother and your father? Your father's upbringing may have influenced how he viewed and treated his wife. If possible, ask older relatives about the ethnic background and culture of the family. Research the culture through books and movies. If your ethnic roots are not strong, consider your mother's home region of the United States and that cultural influence on her life.

We all belong to a certain era in time, whether we typify it or run counter to it. Did our mothers grow up during the

Depression or go to work in the war factories of the 1940s? Were they devoted housewives of the 1950s or flower children of the 1960s? Certainly the times into which our mothers were born and matured were not the only influence on our lives. But the historical context does explain much about what forces and events shaped our mothers' lives.

In the Time Machine

- Research the era in which your mother matured. What were the issues women of her generation faced? Consider too her socioeconomic standing. The concerns of working-class women a generation ago were more immediate than those of wealthier women, who could devote themselves to causes.

- Read a book or watch a movie that depicts accurately your mother's era when she was in her early twenties or a young wife and mother. Look at how women were portrayed and the images that were used to influence and manipulate them.

- Look at a magazine from the year that your mother would have been about twenty-one years old. Libraries, vintage shops and specialty catalogs often have a variety of old magazines available. Even a casual glance at the pages may reveal volumes about society's views of women at that time and how our mothers regarded themselves and other women.

Our mothers' stories reveal much about these women who came before us. Even stories we've heard dozens of times can suddenly enlighten us when we listen differently, when we look beyond the narrative to the themes and lessons they contain.

6

Honoring Our Other Mothers

Even if you had the most wonderful mother
in the world, you may eventually have more than one.
As I have often told my own daughters,
"You are born to one mother, but if you are lucky,
you will have more than one. And among them all
you will find most of what you need."

—CLARISSA PINKOLA ESTES, *WOMEN WHO RUN WITH THE WOLVES*

*W*e had no choice of the mother to whom we were born. We may believe, at least philosophically, that the family in which we grew up was the best for us in light of the life lessons we had to learn. Or we may see our mothers as the perfect women to have raised us, among the true treasures of our lives. Perhaps we view them more stoically, seeing them as good women who, for all their human faults, did the best they could. Or we may still harbor such anger and resentment over their mothering of us that we would have traded them for anyone and anything else, including an inanimate object.

For better or for worse, these were the women who gave birth to us or, in the case of adoption, raised us from infancy. But they were not the only mothers we have ever had or will ever know. Each of us has had "other mothers" in our lives— nurturing, positive and loving people who took care of us physically or emotionally, imparted wisdom or merely loved us for what we were. Chances are, many of us have been "other mothers" ourselves, whether or not we have children of our own, to our siblings and friends.

Being an "other mother" does not depend upon age or genetic link. It is a matter of the heart. In some cases, other mothers came into our lives out of necessity. Our own mothers had died or were emotionally or physically unable to care for us. Some daughters were abandoned on the proverbial doorstep of their grandmothers, who quickly became their mothers. Others experienced a supplemental mothering at key times in their lives, even if they had a warm and emotionally healthy relationship with their own mothers.

We acknowledge the women who have been our "other mothers" in the past, women who raised us themselves or supplemented the nurturing we received.

For women whose mothers have died, the existence of other mothers, past and present, is a blessing. When we acknowledge the women who have mothered us in the past, we open ourselves up to more mothering now—regardless of whether we are gray-haired grandmothers or young women of twenty. When it is mothering that we crave, we can identify the need and go find it. It is our birthright. It is our due. When we need to be mothered, a mother will appear.

But what, we may ask ourselves, do these other mothers have to do with our own deceased mothers, with whom we are trying to connect? If we begin to honor and associate with other women, won't that take away from our relationships with our own mothers? Not at all. The existence of other mothers in our lives helps us to recall the positive mothering we received from the women who gave birth to us. In the case of troubled and traumatic relationships, as we walk the Path of Understanding to grapple with the events and circumstances in our mothers' lives, we are comforted by the memory of others who loved and nurtured us.

The Dessert Parable

Here is an example that, while it may appear silly, helps illustrate the point. Let's say you come to my house for coffee and homemade blueberry pie. You enjoy the first bite and the second, purposely eating slowly to savor the treat. Then it hits you. Why, this dessert is just like Mother used to make! She made *the* best blueberry pie (cherry cobbler, apple strudel or whatever), you recall as you take the next bite. Finishing the last morsel, and resisting the temptation to run your finger over the crumbs on the plate, you sigh contentedly. You enjoyed a delicious dessert and you recalled the fabulous pastry your mother used to make.

Think about it again. You enjoyed an experience in the here and now, and you recalled past pleasures. One invoked the other, and both were honored. And since both were delicious, it was not a choice of one over the other. In the same way, when we experience being mothered by someone else, it recalls the positive experiences we received from our own mothers.

Now to continue our dessert parable, let's say your mother made lousy pie, soggy strudel and gummy cobbler. She couldn't cook worth a damn. You understand why, of course. She was too worn out by all the problems in the family, too sick to have the energy or too defeated by depression to even try. So when you eat a wonderful dessert, you recall another woman: your best friend's mother, who made pastry that could win a blue ribbon at any county fair. No doubt about it, you say to yourself as you enjoy a generous serving of blueberry pie, when it came to baking, your mother was lacking. But thank goodness you had your best friend's mother in your life.

In this instance, our mothers were deficient in giving us the kind of nurturing we craved. On the Path of Understanding, viewing our mothers as women, we can clearly see the circumstances of our mothers' lives. We know that illness, depression or family stresses kept them from being the kind of mothers we wanted them to be. But as in the case of our best friend's mother, the champion baker, we turned to other mothers in our lives for nurturing. We understand our mothers as women, and we acknowledge the existence of others in our lives who gave us mothering that our biological mothers could not.

Seeing ourselves as "motherless" puts us in a state of inextricable sorrow.

Whether we had wonderful or traumatic relationships with our deceased mothers, or a combination of both, it is essential that we do not now see ourselves as motherless. That state of inextricable sorrow does not serve us; it only cripples us emotionally and personally. Surely after our mothers' deaths, in the initial stages of grief, we felt a part of our own bodies was gone. We suffered an indescribable pain. But now, as we move into the next stages of our lives, if we perceive that the sole source of our nurturing is gone, we will mourn the rest of our lives. And if we see ourselves as *never* having been mothered, we will despair. Moreover, the perception of being motherless is a cruel myth, a lie. There are and will be many people in our lives who love and nurture us, if we let them. We begin by honoring the other mothers we have known thus far.

When Mother Is Gone

For many of us, the "other mother" of our lives is our grand-mother, and often the mother of own mother. In some cases, our grandmother was a supplemental caregiver, an older, wiser and sometimes softer pair of arms to cradle our infant bodies and hug our childish ones. In other cases, our grandmothers were the only mothers we knew. For a variety of reasons, including death or abandonment, our biological mothers were unable to care for us. That's when an older woman stepped to the foreground to take responsibility for us—the child, the teenager or the young woman who needed her care.

Whether that grandmother is alive or deceased, recalling and honoring her nurturing is an essential step. We daughters must "own" every bit of mothering we have received. It is key to seeing ourselves as having been validated by another, of being worthy of love.

ॐ

As a baby, Susan was left with her grandmother by her mother, a teenager who could not handle the responsibility of raising an infant. Her birth mother is still alive, although Susan, at age thirty-one, views her more as a sibling as she tries to pursue a relationship with her. The true mother of her life, the one who nurtured and cared for her, was Grandmother Pearl.

Grandmother Pearl, a Native American who spent much of her life in Kentucky, gave Susan the gift of a heritage, teaching her to speak Cherokee, Navajo and a little Spanish that she picked up along the way. Although Grandmother Pearl never went beyond the fourth grade, she had a sharp, inquisitive mind and valued education. She ran a strict household but believed in music and dancing. "I grew up with a combination of Mahalia Jackson, Hank Williams Sr. and Elvis," Susan laughs.

Grandmother Pearl knew the value of a good sense of humor and the ability to let insults roll off one's back. "We were called prairie trash, which I didn't understand as a kid," Susan says. "My grandmother never lowered herself to respond. She'd pull herself up— she was only five feet tall—and she would never talk about people's comments with anger."

When Grandmother Pearl was dying of breast cancer, Susan left college to care for her. "I found that she still had much to teach me and our bond grew even more," Susan says in her Web page dedicated to her grandmother. "Our nights were filled with her telling me stories of our culture and of her life and mine as well." (To view Susan's "Spirit of Pearl" tribute go to her home page at *http://geocities.com/Wellesley/2619/* and select the "Spirit of Pearl" link.)

It is little wonder that Susan considers Grandmother Pearl to be an angelic presence in her life now, watching over and guarding her. For daughters who were not "mothered" by the women who gave birth to them, the presence of other, nurturing women in their lives is essential for their personal development.

The existence of "other mothers"
in our lives is essential to all women. The need is
most critical for daughters who were rejected or
inadequately nurtured by their mothers.

"The 'other mothers' are hugely important," says psychologist Dr. Joyce Fraser, who specializes in women's issues. For women who perceived themselves as having been rejected by their mothers, those who experienced any kind of nurturing—including from their fathers—do better in life than those who felt they lacked all mothering.

Dr. Fraser, whose mother was an alcoholic, is among the women she considers to have been "unmothered daughters," the topic of her doctoral thesis. But there were positive female role models in her life when she was growing up, Dr. Fraser recalls. "We had a housekeeper when I was growing up who was like my mother."

When We Had Two Mothers

There are times when we feel as though we had two mothers: the one who gave birth to us and another woman, often a relative, who raised us. Our own mother, because of illness or tragic circumstance, could not handle the job of raising us alone. Another woman came into our lives to act as a second mother. Looking back, we may feel our loyalties were divided or that we favored one over the other. As children, however, we were not equipped to choose or make that judgment. We needed mothering and gravitated to the sources of nurturing available to us. As adults, looking to understand our mothers as women, we begin to unravel a tangle of relationships. But at the heart is the kernel of truth: We were loved and nurtured.

≥ξ

Debra was rescued by her grandmother. Her mother, tragically, had a mental breakdown because of a failed marriage that entrapped her, and was unable to act as a mother to Debra.

"With no way out and no way in, she quite frankly found her 'place' in madness," Debra explains. "And so began my journey as the 'crazy lady's daughter.' What saved me, what made me who I am, the sane daughter—and I have questioned my whole life the meaning of sanity—was my grandmother's unconditional love."

For her grandmother, raising Debra was a second chance at motherhood and an avenue of healing. Her grandmother had lost a child in the influenza epidemic of 1918, a loss from which she never recovered. "Not until I arrived thirty years later, her surrogate child, did she begin to recover," Debra says. "Until my grandmother's death when I was eleven, she was my mother, earning my respect and my own unconditional love."

In retrospect, Debra sees that although she called her mother Mommy, she never came to love her as her primary caregiver. Her mother was inept at mothering, and her frequent hospitalizations gave her little opportunity to learn parenting skills. Now, Debra sorts through the relationships of her early life, understanding both the circumstances and the choices of her mother's and her grandmother's lives. And, as the Path of Understanding inevitably leads us, she contemplates her own life as a writer.

"In words, I have found the sanity my mother was denied," Debra states. "And in the end, it is through words that I hope to reclaim my mother's life. As with all female children, my mother lives in me. Both of my mothers."

Daughters may also experience having had two mothers because of divorce or the early death of their birth mothers. Sister Mercedes Ventencilla, a member of the Order of the Columban Sisters in Manila, had a loving relationship with her birth mother before she died and then with her step-mother after her father remarried. While both relationships were strong and positive, neither one overshadowed the other. From Sister Mercedes' point of view, she had two mothers—one who gave birth to her and raised her to about the age of ten, and one who nurtured her into adulthood.

"Other mothers" are powerful contributors to our development, even if we had strong and nurturing relationships with our own mothers.

The Extended Family

Even when relationships between mothers and daughters were good, the presence of "other mothers" was a powerful contributor to the development of our womanhood. Perhaps it was an older sister, an aunt or a grandmother who helped to nurture us. In our culture today, we may not value this role as much as we should. We live scattered lives, geographically and psychologically. We don't have time to gather as an extended family as we once did. And when we do get together, we may all be a little too crazed by whatever else is happening in our frantic lives to feel the connection.

But there was a time (and with a little effort there can be again) when extended family meant just that. Our nucleus of parents and children extended to include others of the same— or honorary—bloodlines. Mothers, grandmothers and aunts doled out hugs and scoldings on an equal basis. They helped to raise us, sometimes by living in the same house or at least the same neighborhood. We took their presence for granted as children because they were such a part of our lives. These women were closer to us than the title of "aunt" and "grandmother" convey. They were extensions of our mothers and of the nurturing we received.

"Relationships between women, whether the women share the same bloodlines or are psychic soul mates, whether the relationship is between analyst and patient, between teacher and apprentice, or between kindred spirits, are kinship relationships of the most important kind," author and psychologist Clarissa Pinkola Estés writes in *Women Who Run with the Wolves: Myths and Stories of the Wild Woman Archetype.*

For Kim, her grandmother's apartment on the South Side of Chicago was a second home, a supplement to where she lived, happily, with her parents. As close as Kim was and is with her mother, there was always a special bond with her maternal grandmother, who had been raised in a working-class African-American family in Mississippi and who worked as a private-duty nurse in Chicago.

Kim, an aspiring filmmaker, attributes her avocation to her grandmother, now deceased. She had loved theater and the arts, and had infused this same passion in Kim. "My grandmother believed in getting the best things in life. I called her Miss Entertainment. She loved to cook and put out all the silver and china," Kim says.

Kim considers herself lucky to have had two role models in her life—her mother, whom she sees as "mom/girlfriend/sister," and her grandmother, who taught her the value of a close family and of being independent.

Looking back on my life, I see so many other mothers. With some, I have had a long-term relationship, while with others it is a closeness born of necessity and circumstance. My aunts, a group of strong, wise and loving women, were role models as wives and mothers when I was growing up. My mother's younger sister, Aunt Jeanne, was an "other mother" right from the start. She and her two children, my cousins Michelene and Peter, lived with my grandparents just two houses away. Not only were Aunt Jeanne and my mother close as sisters and friends, but in many ways to us children they were extensions of each other.

In my early twenties, Aunt Jeanne became a confidante— sometimes to my mother's dismay, when she longed for a closer relationship with me. But there are simply things a young woman can talk about with an aunt that she does not want to discuss with a mother—like men and relationships and sex.

*My Aunt Jeanne, an "other mother" to me
for most of my life, has always been someone with
whom I could talk about life, about hopes and
dreams, and lately about my mother.*

It was more than that—although I know I will embarrass Aunt Jeanne to say this publicly. She was simply more hip than my mother. My mother, for all her fun and frolic, was very strict and rather rigid. Aunt Jeanne was more broad-minded. Now, I've never heard my aunt say the kind of four-letter word that would get a movie an "R" rating and we've never had anything stronger to drink together than coffee. But we could talk—about life, about hopes and dreams, and lately, about my mother. I treasure the chance to get to know my mother through my "other mother" who lived just down the road.

Our lives are populated with other mothers if we only look. I turn to a defining line in *Women Who Run with the Wolves*: "Your relationships with *todas las madres*, the many mothers, will most likely be ongoing ones, for the need for guidance and advisory is never outgrown, nor, from the point of view of women's deep creative life, should it ever be."

As the wise aunt, the listening friend
and the nurturing sister, we join the circle of
"other mothers" of the world.

From this heritage springs our own roles as "other mothers." Each time we act as the wise aunt, the listening friend, the nurturing sister, we step into the roles of "other motherhood." On Thanksgiving 1997, I was blessed with the chance to dole out a little wise advice about boys and dating to my dear friend's teenage daughter, who calls me "Aunt Tricia." I say that I was blessed because during that hour or so that we talked I took my place among *"todas las madres"*—the many mothers. We are, I believe, spiritual mothers and daughters for all of our lives, giving and receiving nurturing.

"She asked for a pecan pie. That was her favorite and I made it for her."

When I heard those words spoken by the woman in the booth behind me in the restaurant where I was eating breakfast with my son, I couldn't help listening to the rest of the story. (This is my second confession of eavesdropping for the sake of my research, a habit I'm afraid I'm likely to continue.)

The woman explained to her companion that when she was a teacher, she always baked a cake for her students' birthdays. But one girl, she recalled, asked for a pecan pie. "When I made it, she was so happy," the woman said. "She told me that no one had ever made a pie for her before."

I smiled at the story, recognizing another tale of "other motherhood," in this instance from a teacher. I do not know why the girl's mother had never made her a pie, but I silently thanked the woman behind me for extending that kindness. And I hope that, somewhere out there, a woman remembers the pecan pie her teacher once baked as she contemplates the "other mothers" of her life.

The First Nurturing

The memories of all those who loved and nurtured us, from our birth mothers to our other mothers, affirm the fact that we were cherished and validated by others in our lives. Recalling this past mothering, we also open ourselves to the chance to experience it again. In fact, there are times in our lives when only a mother will do. We reach out for ours and, if she is not there physically, we connect with her spiritually and psychologically. But it does not end there. Through our connection with our mothers we can seek out "other mothers" as well.

An inner-ear infection had knocked out my equilibrium to the point that, each time I moved my head, waves of nausea rolled over me. I could not sit up or stand without vomiting. I had to get to the doctor, but driving was out of the question. I could have called a taxi or asked my husband to come home from work. But the person I wanted to take care of me in this vulnerable condition was my mother. Under the circumstances, that was out of the question.

But there was an "other mother" nearby, my dear neighbor Betty, who kindly drove me to the doctor, played with my son in the waiting room while the doctor examined me, and then drove me home. A mother of four and grandmother of eight, Betty became my "other mother" for that afternoon. In her kindness and caring, she helped me remember and connect with the first mother I ever knew who, if she were alive, would have done the same things for me.

There was a time in my life when I would never have called someone like Betty to help me. I would have taken a taxi or, worse still, struggled to drive myself to the doctor, feverishly clutching the steering wheel while willing myself not to throw up. For many years after my mother's death, I saw myself as cut off from that nurturing and therefore unable to tap into mothering of any sort. Then I started on the Path of Understanding to get to know my mother again, reconnecting with her so many years after her death. The unexpected development in this journey is that not only do I feel the love my mother had for me, but I have found nurturing and mothering from other sources in my life as well.

Men as "Other Mothers"

We may tend to think of our "other mothers" along gender lines; we may believe that since only women can biologically be mothers, only women can be "other mothers." That is, thankfully, not the case. Men, in particular fathers and grandfathers, can often take on a nurturing role that we associate with mothering.

---

*Men, in particular fathers and grandfathers,
can also play a nurturing role in our lives, becoming our
"other mothers" in spite of the gender difference.*

After my mother died, my father became more emotionally involved in our lives, even though my sisters and I were adults at the time. Dad, who had been the traditional 1950s bread-winner when we were growing up, did not stop being the father. He assumed a more nurturing, "mothering" role as well.

Looking back at our childhoods, we may find we were nur-tured by men as well as women. My sister, Jeannie, recalls that when she was growing up, she enjoyed a special relationship with our maternal grandfather. I did not know Grandpa well; he died when I was ten. But Jeannie was nineteen at that time, and had grown into young adulthood with Grandpa playing a key role in her life. When she speaks of Grandpa, it is clear that he was an "other mother" for her.

❧

"Grandpa was my best friend. He was my encyclopedia because he knew so many things. I saw everything in the world through his eyes," says Jeannie, now forty-seven.

For Jeannie, Grandpa was a teacher of things like how to fish, how to parallel-park a car and how to appreciate nature. "He taught me how to see trees, plants, blades of grass, all living things and to appreciate them. There was no such thing as a weed or a blemish on the earth in Grandpa's eyes."

Grandpa, though crippled by arthritis, never stopped moving in the world, although his pace was as slow as a crawl. He went everywhere he could, driving a four-door Bonneville and an old John Deere tractor with equal ease. On many of these excursions, he had Jeannie at his side. Other times she would be at the workshop he kept in the old barn, a place that smelled of dust and turpentine and wood shavings. Here he made things like bookshelves and picture frames for his watercolor paintings. And here, he would talk to Jeannie about life.

"He turned to me once and said, 'Little Jeannie, some day you are going to get married. Even if your husband is a poor man, that does not matter. It's only if you cannot find peace, contentment and happiness when you look at your backyard that you will be poor,'" recalls Jeannie, who has been married to Ben for nearly twenty-four years.

Today, Jeannie is an artist like her grandfather, but works in the medium of fabric and quilting. She sees Grandpa as a guiding presence in her life. "Grandpa, I strongly believe, is my guardian angel," she says.

That brings me to another source of mothering, one that we may underestimate and undervalue: ourselves. For all of us, part of becoming self-actualized adults means we have internalized our parenting. We have cast off the negative influences and absorbed the positive ones. We take care of ourselves because we recognize that we are worth it. We feel validated because we view ourselves that way. When we are sick, we tuck ourselves into bed an hour earlier without a thought to the laundry or paperwork that beckons. We praise ourselves for jobs well done.

We carry within ourselves "internal mothers"
who reflect our relationships with our actual mothers
and the "other mothers" of our lives.

This is what psychologists refer to as the internal mother, the inner parent we carry around with us for all our lives. "This internal mother is made from not only the experiences of the personal mother but also other mothering figures in our lives, as well as the images held out as the good mother and the bad mother in the culture at the time of our childhoods," Clarissa Pinkola Estés writes.

Making Peace with Our "Internal Mothers"

On the Path of Understanding, when we view our mothers as women, we may find that our internal mother has softened. The shrill criticism no longer rings in our ears; we have let go of the resentment we felt for our mothers, and of their anger that we internalized. Seeing our mothers as the flawed human beings that they were, and that we all are, we find our internal mother has become more broad-minded, gentle and accepting. Through understanding, we are at peace with our mothers and our internal mothers as well. Now we can love and nurture ourselves as the wondrous, beautiful creatures that we are.

This healing progression reminds us that reconnecting with our mothers by understanding them as women is a journey. The destination, ultimately, is one of self-love and -acceptance. It is impossible, I believe, to have one without the other. Loving and accepting ourselves for what we are, we must be at peace with where we came from. Being at peace with our mothers, the women who came before us, we learn to love and accept ourselves.

When I started this project, I knew that I could never fully understand myself as a woman until I understood my mother from the same perspective. What I did not realize until much later was that I would learn more about myself in the year that I worked on this book than I had since my mother died. The more I pursued a connection with my mother, the more I came to know myself. As I understood my mother's faults and frailties, I came to see my own failings, but without the harsh judgment of perfection.

Perhaps that was the biggest payoff of all. Allowing my mother to be human, I gave myself the same permission. Seeing her as imperfect, I no longer demanded that I live up to super-human standards in order to be loved. I no longer saw love as the prize for some contest of virtue, but rather as my birthright as a human being. I accepted as truth the fact that I had been loved by my mother as best as she could and by many "other mothers" as well, who supplemented and continued my mother's legacy of nurturing. In that, other mothers are a gift—consciously or unconsciously—from our mothers, and through them, from God.

Allowing my mother to be human,
I gave myself the same permission.

Perhaps it is a fantasy of mine, but I would like to think that our mothers continue to love us through the people in our lives today. On a psychological level, I know that having had parents who loved me allows me to accept love in my life today. On a spiritual level, I believe the great mother-love flows from an eternal Source. That love is a gift that is not forced upon us, but rather one that must be accepted. The form it comes in may vary, from a mother's arms or a father's gentle touch to the loving presence of others. But the gift awaits us, eternally and abundantly offered.

Connections

The "other mothers" of our lives do not replace the woman who gave birth to us, even if she died soon after we were born. No matter the circumstances of our lives, our first mother is the woman who carried us in her womb and from whom we came into the world. Yet there were other mothers in our lives who either supplemented the nurturing we received or were the sole source of it. They were grandmothers, aunts, older sisters and the mothers of friends. They appeared in our childhood, our teen years, the day we got married and when we bought the first house. Whether our mothers are alive or dead, these "other mothers" are in our lives now and will be in the future.

The Other Mothers

- Think of all the women who acted as "other mothers" in your life. Remember the aunts who took you to the beach when your mother had to work or was busy with younger siblings. Recall your best friend's mother who treated you like another daughter. Think back to the woman, an older sister or a young aunt, who taught you about makeup and men. Make a list of all the "other mothers" of the past, and then all the women—and men—who play a nurturing role in your life now.

- If there is a special "other mother" in your life, honor that relationship. If she is still alive, write a letter or make a phone call to tell her how much you would like to renew that connection. If she is deceased, do something in her memory, from baking your favorite cake that she always made for you to lighting a candle or saying a prayer.

No matter how far we've come in our lives, how at peace we feel with our mothers and ourselves, or how much time has passed since our mothers died, there are often times of lingering sadness when we miss her more than we dare admit to ourselves. One such time, for obvious reasons, is Mother's Day. Even if we are mothers ourselves, receiving cards and gifts from our own children and grandchildren, many of us feel a pinch of pain that we are not sending a card to our mothers. On the Path of Understanding, pursuing a spiritual and psychological link with our mothers, we allow ourselves to feel that sadness. We recognize it as a sign that we need to bring the essence of our mothers into our lives again. But in the here and now, when it is mothering we need—a physical hug or a word of assurance— we give ourselves permission to seek out another mother.

Happy Mother's Day

- In honor of your mother, on the next Mother's Day send cards to the "other mothers" who nurtured you. This past Mother's Day, I sent cards to my mother's two sisters in her memory. This year, I will send cards to all my aunts. I am not looking for them to replace or become my mother. Rather, I am honoring a connection that exists between us in honor of the mother I had. Even women whose mothers are still alive can take time to honor these other special women in their lives.

- In times of stress, seek out an "other mother." Look for a nurturing, loving person who can help you over the rough spots. This is not to turn ourselves into children, but rather to allow ourselves to receive mothering.

- In times of happiness, share your joy with an "other mother." This is especially important if your "other mother" has seen you through the bad times as well. Call up that nurturing person in your life when the promotion comes through, the house sells or your child makes the honor roll at school.

We are all called to be other mothers at times in our lives. Our nieces, our friend's children, our students or a young woman on an airplane may look to us for nurturing and guidance—for an hour or a lifetime. When we take on the role of a healthy "other mother," we join the circle of wise women that descend from Eve.

- Think about the times you have been an "other mother." What were the circumstances? Did your niece confide in you? Did a friend's daughter turn to you when her mother was ill? What "other mother" relationships exist in your life right now?

- Is there anyone in your family or within your circle of friends who needs an "other mother"? Offer your listening ear and your loving guidance. Of course, we don't want to turn the person into an emotional cripple who is unhealthily dependent upon us. But when we offer our love and support, we become an "other mother."

- Is there a volunteer organization that brings out your desire to be an "other mother"? Is there a group dedicated to women and children that needs your help? A donation of our time, money or something we no longer use fulfills a need in us to extend ourselves, and benefits society as well.

Within each of us there is an internal mother to whom we have given birth. She was formed by our relationship with our own mother, as well as by the mother images of our culture. Our internal mother is that echo in our minds that chastises us, sometimes harshly, or praises us for our accomplishments. As we are at peace with our mothers, understanding them as women, our internal mothers soften. As we accept all of who we are, we let go of the anger and resentment that our internal mothers have harbored for years. We allow ourselves to feel loved because we are more loving toward ourselves.

Listening to "Mother"

- What does your "internal mother" have to say about you? Do you feel validated and loved? Or does your internal mother criticize and insult you? If your internal mother is not a gentle voice, chances are she reflects unresolved anger and conflict with your mother. In the case of a bitter or cruel internal mother, it is time to find out why she acts the way she does.

- Think about what your "internal mother" is saying to you. Take note if she criticizes your appearance, your lack of a better job, or your choice of life partner. Does your internal mother reflect what you, yourself, honestly think? If so, what steps are you willing to take to address these issues? If not, it's time to confront your "internal mother" and to tell her that you are quite capable of making your own life choices.

- As you walk the Path of Understanding to get to know your own mother, chances are your internal mother will become a kinder, gentler presence. In a meditative moment, contemplate what you have learned about your mother as an individual. What insights have you gained into her life and personality? What conflict with your mother has been resolved by understanding her as a woman? Bring that understanding into yourself and incorporate it into your internal mother. As you experience love and acceptance of your mother, your internal mother will respond.

We are not motherless, whether we are teenagers or in our eighties. A connection exists with our mothers that extends far beyond death. And other mothers—those positive, nurturing people who gave us the validation we needed and the love we craved—existed in our pasts and are available to us now. All we have to do is look and ask.

7

Messages from Beyond

Once someone passes out of the world
of the physical and into the world of the spiritual,
we can never physically experience them again the way
we once knew. But we can always experience them and
have them share in our lives by keeping their memories
alive in our minds and hearts and by realizing that,
as spiritual beings not limited to physical properties,
they are more often around us than ever before.

—JAMES VAN PRAAGH, *TALKING TO HEAVEN:*
A MEDIUM'S MESSAGE OF LIFE AFTER DEATH

*W*here do we go after we die? It is a question we ponder throughout our lives, especially when someone
we love dies. Think of the words we use to euphemistically
describe death: pass on, pass away. They connote a journey
of some sort, leaving here for there —wherever there is. Our

religious faith and philosophic beliefs give us some insight into what we believe exists after this life, whether it be reincarnation or the communion of saints in heaven. We may not even be able to verbalize our feelings about the after-life, other than to believe that our earthly existence is not the end. Something lives on, most of us believe. Somewhere. Somehow.

For many of us, our proof is grounded in our religious faith, which we find reflected in the Talmud, the Koran or the Bible. Yet there is another reflection of faith in experiences that we hold tightly inside ourselves, sharing with only those few who would understand and believe. These experiences may be dreams or visions or sounds, coincidences or miracles. But we know what they are when they happen to us, and no one can dissuade us from our belief. They are messages from beyond, a soothing reassurance that while our mothers are not here, they are not gone forever. And, perhaps more important, that we have not been forgotten.

When I first began writing this book, I wondered if I would truly gather enough of these stories to have a whole chapter on "messages from beyond." I quickly discovered that many women had experiences of the uncanny—if not the supernatural—variety that they ascribed to their mothers. I had my own experience just recently, a glimpse of my mother that I hold so dear, I will never doubt or forget it. My own experience confirms for me what other women have told me: our mothers continue to love us. After death, in a place of spiritual perfection, our mothers can love us the way they were unable to on earth.

I am neither theologian, mystic nor psychologist, although all three fields fascinate me. It is not in my power or my purpose to persuade someone to embrace one belief and discard another. I cannot prove the existence of an afterlife to those who doubt, or argue the nature of heaven with those who believe. I only know what I was taught as a child and the beliefs I have refined as an adult: that this earthly existence is not all there is. Our life in this moment is not the end of the line. We begin, as souls, elsewhere, a state of being to which we return. I call it heaven, a place of eternal connection with God. That, I believe, is where my mother rests.

There are times when the distance between heaven and earth seems to narrow.

Narrowing the Distance to Heaven

I remember someone explaining to me years ago that God is love and that because God is eternal, love is eternal. In our relationships with our mothers and the "other mothers" of our lives, where there has been love, it will continue to exist. Sometimes this love manifests itself in a feeling that we are not alone even in an empty room or when life suddenly takes a difficult turn. That is when heaven does not seem too distant from earth, when the spiritual tie between the two realms is tangible.

We feel a touch or a presence; we smell flowers or the scent of a nearly forgotten perfume. We are saved from a trauma, or find the strength to endure one. Many women, including myself, have had these experiences. I share here some of the stories that were told to me. The stories come from both women who follow an organized religion—Christianity, Judaism or Buddhism—and those who do not. Regardless of their religious or philosophic beliefs, the women describe experiences that are amazingly similar in form and in message: Our mothers' love and caring for us do not end with this life.

Some might say these experiences boil down to wishful thinking, some psychological need to feel an ongoing connection with one's deceased mother. If that is the case, I still cherish these stories. Even if our subconscious minds conjured up these images and experiences, they are precious in that they show how deeply integrated our mother connections are with our psyches. If our experiences of the loving, angelic presence of our mothers comes only from ourselves, I still wholeheartedly embrace them. They reflect that, at the core, we know and accept our mothers' love.

Some women may feel uneasy with these stories because of their religious beliefs. Dreams, visions and voices may smack too much of spiritualism for them. Again, it is not my place to prove or disprove, but I note that many of us believe that our loved ones in death are united with God. Since God is everpresent, so are those who are joined with him.

These stories carry messages not only of enduring love but also of hope. We who cling so closely to this life need not be afraid of what comes next. There will be light and love to welcome us.

Some believe that death is not to be feared.
It is not a punishment or the end of the game, but
rather, the goal of this life. It is the doorway
to pass to the next life.

Death as a Passage

We don't like the idea of dying since it usually involves sickness and pain. We know we are mortal, but we try to focus on living in the moment, being in the here and now. We do not stop to ponder the last moment, going to the then and there. But some believe that death is not to be feared. They don't view it as a punishment or the inevitable end of the game. They see death as the goal of this life, the doorway through which we pass from this life of pain and sacrifice into the next one of spiritual fulfillment and bliss.

Dr. Elisabeth Kübler-Ross, the Swiss-born psychiatrist and author, changed the way the medical profession treated dying patients with her breakthrough book, *On Death and Dying*. In her latest and last book, *The Wheel of Life: A Memoir of Living and Dying*, she speaks candidly of her life's work with dying patients and her spiritual quest that led to her unshakable belief in the afterlife. I had a chance to interview Dr. Kübler-Ross in her home in the Arizona desert in September 1997. After having suffered two strokes and partial paralysis, Dr. Kübler-Ross stated very calmly that she was dying, although she did not know how long the process would take. I asked her if she was afraid.

"You must be kidding," she replied. "That's the joke of the century. After working with dying patients for half a century, I can't wait. There is nothing to be afraid of," she added.

Dr. Kübler-Ross also believed that the souls in the next life helped those of us in this one; she believed in angels and saints—or guides, as she called them—that assisted us in our journeys in this life. She told the story of giving a lecture and being asked about dying children, a subject that most of us find too painful to even contemplate. She became aware suddenly of a presence, which Dr. Kübler-Ross knew was the Virgin Mary. "She gave me answers and ideas that would never have come to my head if it hadn't been for her," she recalled.

After that, when she was lecturing she would receive a sign: a pink rose that would be placed anonymously on the speaker's podium. She interpreted this as a signal from Mary that she should speak about dying children. "Every time I had a pink rose I knew I had to talk about dying children. And then in the audience people would get up and say they had dying children. . . ."

It is a matter of faith, of course, whether we consider experiences such as Dr. Kübler-Ross's coincidences or a message from the next life. All I know from my own life is that there is a spiritual side to everything, that every experience carries a potential spiritual lesson. We can choose to live with our minds and hearts open to the experience, or dismiss it as delusional. I have chosen a path of openness by desire as much as by necessity, looking for comfort and proof. As I began researching this book, I discovered I was not alone on that walk.

The stories of these "messages from beyond" almost always begin the same way: "You're probably not going to believe this, but . . ." Then I know what will follow: a story that the woman is both embarrassed and eager to share. But the experiences these women describe are so real, they have no choice but to believe. The belief that their mothers have died in an earthly sense, but now inhabit a spiritual realm, brings peace and hope. We can view death as a passage and not an endless abyss.

Connecting Through Dreams

*In dreams, we see her face and hear her voice.
It is not like any other dream, but rather feels like a
visitation. We awaken with a feeling that we
have seen her and that she has delivered
to us a powerful message.*

For many of us, a spiritual connection with our mothers is fostered by dreams. Dreams are important. Psychiatrists and psychoanalysts spend a lot of time helping their patients explore and interpret their dreams. In history and in literature, we are told of life-changing and prophetic dreams. We recall the stories in the Bible of St. Joseph, worried that Mary is with child, receiving a dream in which he is told that her child was conceived through the power of God. After the birth of Christ, Joseph was told in a dream to flee from Herod into Egypt.

But when are dreams more than just a mini-mental movie, entertaining or enlightening? What happens if we feel we've been outside ourselves, or that someone has come into our sleeping minds? Psychics believe strongly that in dreams, we dwell in a union of a greater unconsciousness where we can, indeed, contact others.

"Many people have asked if it is possible to reach those who have passed over through dreams. The answer is an unequivocal YES! The spirit body leaves the physical body every night when we go to sleep," James Van Praagh, a renowned spiritual medium, writes in his bestselling book, *Talking to Heaven: A Medium's Message of Life After Death.*

*If we perceive spiritual help from outside of ourselves,
or if these experiences are produced by our own
unconscious minds, we are equally blessed.*

Mother Dreams

What makes some dreams different from others is the message that is delivered. We awaken with a peacefulness, knowing that our mothers are in a place of contentment and beauty. We no longer worry about our mothers, although that brief glimpse of them may leave us hungry for yet another. These dreams release us from our fears and anxiety with a message that our mothers are okay; they have gone to a place of beauty and peace. No longer worried about them, our own troubled spirits can rest.

On a psychological level, the dreams reveal that we have processed the impact of our mothers' deaths and have come to terms with our own grieving. From a spiritual perspective, our beliefs are strengthened by an inner knowledge that our mothers live on in a place that we cannot see with our eyes, but that is real to us nonetheless.

❧

Sandy E. had such a dream after months of mourning her mother and missing her terribly. Curiously, when she shared this story, she prefaced it by saying that she was not the type of person who normally remembered her dreams, let alone analyzed them. But this dream carried such a powerful image, it has stayed with her for more than a dozen years.

A Catholic, Sandy believed her mother was in heaven. But emotionally, she needed assurance that her mother was all right. One night Sandy dreamed of the biggest white stretch limousine she had ever seen. She looked inside and saw it was filled with little cherubs. In the center was her mother, smiling. As the limousine pulled away, Sandy was filled with joy and contentment. "I thought, 'She's okay. She's at peace. She's happy.'"

Since that dream, Sandy says that while she misses her mother, she does not worry about where she is. The limousine dream showed her that her mother was in heaven, happy and peaceful. The dream also gave her another gift: an image that recalls that experience each time she sees—in waking hours—a white limousine.

"You wouldn't believe how many times I see a white limousine drive by or parked somewhere. Each time I see one I say to myself, 'Hi, Mom.' It's a nice reminder," Sandy says.

Many women speak of seeing their mothers in dreams that are unlike any others. These are not the usual dreams of people and places, events and happenings. The unique dreams that some of us have experienced are more like a visit during which we see our deceased mothers and listen to or speak with them. We awaken suddenly with the feeling that we have been visited. It is as if a friend had stopped by and then just recently left. Even the air seems different, and we may have trouble going back to sleep because we have been fully awakened. That is what Trisha experienced one night.

❧

In her dream, Trisha saw her mother and father, both deceased, sitting at the foot of her bed. They reached out and took her hands, holding them gently, without saying a word. Upon awakening,

Trisha looked around the room expectantly but saw nothing. Yet her hands felt as though they had been held for a long time. In her dream, Trisha believes, her parents came to her, and in a gentle gesture, showed her that they were together in death as they had been in life; that their love for her would never die.

Often those who have had a dream visitation from their mothers say it came at a time when they most needed help. A crisis in their own lives prompted their mothers to intervene with a word of wisdom, with love and empathy. These stories tell of love and caring that continue beyond the grave, and a belief that we are not separate from our mothers, nor they from us. We have not been abandoned or forgotten.

Janie was alone and lonely. To outsiders, she had it all—good looks, intelligence, a successful career, and a chance to live in Asia at a time of great historic change: the protest at Tiananmen Square. But at the heart of her existence were isolation, loneliness and grief for her mother, who had recently died. Then a man with whom she had a platonic relationship asked her to marry him. It was an escape route that Janie was tempted to take. "I think between grieving for Mother, the exhaustion of the job and living in a very foreign place, I wasn't thinking clearly," Janie recalls. "I was tempted to say yes."

Then one night, about a year after her mother's death, Janie had a remarkable dream.

"It was a very brief dream, and it seemed more like a visitation than a dream. I saw a very filmy kind of image of Mother—I couldn't see the bottom of her, just the top three-quarters—hovering at the base of my bed. All she said was, 'I know what it's like to be your age and to believe that there will never be anyone for you.' And that was all. When I woke up, I was 100 percent clear that I was not going to marry (the man who proposed) and I was 100 percent clear that I would meet and marry the man of my life. I felt that dream was a specific message from her," Janie says. "She was speaking from a place of knowledge that she had gained in her life. She had waited until the age of thirty-six to get married. It was the kind of message that could only come from her."

Less than two years later Janie would, indeed, meet the man of her life, thanks to a series of events that she ascribes to her mother's loving intervention. When Janie decided to return to the United States, the first professional opportunity offered to her was in Chicago, not far from her small Illinois hometown. Although she resisted at first—she had spent much of her adult life on the East and West coasts—eventually Janie decided to take the job. "At first I thought no, I don't want that," recalls Janie. "Then I woke up the next morning, called my boss and said I wanted the job. I absolutely wanted it. I felt led. I believe there were forces leading me to my destiny." Chicago is where Janie would meet her husband. They are happily married and still live there.

When we share our dreams and spiritual experiences with our intimates, we spread the blessing. Our interpretation of neverending love and a connection beyond the grave extends beyond us to others. Moreover, the sharing of the stories creates a special bond among the living.

Jean, a writer, is very close to her two sons, one in high school and one in college. She sees them as the distinct individuals they are, and tailors her mothering accordingly. Her parenting is different in style from her own strict upbringing with a domineering father and a submissive mother. But there was love in her childhood, which continues in her adulthood and extends to her children, as reflected in her son's dream.

❧

Jean's older son, J., had a dream one night in which he received a telephone call from his grandfather. "I understand that you are unhappy," his grandfather said in the dream. "Come stay with us, and your grandmother and I will make you happy."

In a flash he was with them, embraced by love and acceptance. But even more remarkable was the image in the dream of his grandmother as a sculptor at work on a masterpiece. The sculpture was crystal, about the size of a large egg. Looking through this clear oval, which sat on a slab of polished marble, J. could see what looked like water in the middle.

The dream was so powerful, J. called Jean the next morning to relay it to her. They have discussed its meaning several times, always focusing on Jean's mother, the sculptor. Perhaps she sculpts now the way she shaped their lives, lovingly and patiently. As for mother and son, the dream story forged yet another bond between them in the shared belief that Jean's parents are in a place of beauty and peace. As for the sculpture, J. believes he will find something like it some day.

A Lasting Imprint

From a psychological or spiritual perspective, the dreams reveal an ongoing connection that death cannot break. This connection, psychic and lecturer Linda Dillon believes, is forged in our infancy and acts like a kind of imprint. We all know that ducklings, soon after hatching, become imprinted with the image of the first thing they encounter, which then becomes their "mother." Whatever "Mother" is—another duck, a lab technician in a white coat or a farm dog—the ducklings follow. So, too, were we imprinted in our early days with a mother image that remains for the rest of our lives.

"It is a spiritual, emotional, psychic imprint," Linda explains. "Whether you recognize it or not, it's there. I think that imprint works both ways, both positively and negatively. You need to come to understand who your mother really is, what that imprint is; otherwise you cannot understand yourself."

Images, sounds, scents and sensations recall our mothers.
On a spiritual level these reminders make us
feel that our mothers are reaching out to us.

Even after our mothers' deaths, the imprint does not fade. It remains with us until we die. This imprint, I believe, contains the "calling cards" that remind us of our mothers, such as a particular scent, a song or a place. On one level, those reminders serve as a powerful link in the Call to Connection, often sparking a desire to get to know our mothers again. On another level, these reminders may feel like our mothers are reaching out to us. They take on a spiritual connotation for us.

Emelia told me of the floral scent she sometimes smells in a room that is devoid of flowers. At that moment, she believes the spirit of her mother, a woman of beauty and passion, infuses the room. Other women speak of a feeling that their mothers were "right there" beside them at times, a tangible, physical presence that they could not see. Others have heard a voice, not with their ears but with their minds, that could only be one person—their mothers. They believe, and their faith is unshakable.

A Sacred Journey

The search for connection with our mothers may take us on a journey. Through meditation, or by traveling to a place we believe is sacred, whether it be Tibet or the Cathedral of Notre Dame, we seek peace and serenity from the other side.

Paula, a child psychologist on the East Coast, felt her mother's spiritual presence on the day she died. After receiving the call from the nursing home that her mother had passed away, Paula sat with her mother's body and read Buddhist prayers to help her passage to the next life. "When I started to read this prayer, I heard her say to me, 'Honey, we were not raised Buddhist,'" recalls Paula, who describes herself as being half Catholic, half Buddhist. "So I switched to prayers asking the Blessed Mother to receive her soul."

Even now, two years after her mother's death, Paula says she can still sense her mother's presence. The strongest sensation was when she went to Tibet, on a spiritual journey that became one of rebirth and connection. While there, Paula walked the *Parikrama*, which involved circumnavigating a sacred mountain while meditating and praying—and fearfully fighting off altitude sickness.

"We had been on the trail ten minutes when I felt my mother's physical presence. She was right there through this whole experience," recalls Paula. "She showed up at the beginning when I was scared. She was doing this walk with me."

Before her mother's death, Paula explained, she experienced unconditional love for and from her mother. But on the *Parikrama* she went through another emotional passage, letting go of the power struggle that had marked the relationship between herself and her mother. "So post death, I was really getting a new definition of who she was. I could see her as a sister," she adds.

At the end of a grueling trek out of Tibet, enduring an early monsoon while holed up in tents, the leaders of Paula's trip negotiated a helicopter to rescue the party. At that moment of departure, Paula says she received a powerful message from her mother. "She said, 'You're okay now. I need to spend some time with your brother.'"

With that, Paula and the others left Tibet.

The Help of Angels

Many of us may never experience something as dramatic as Paula's journey to Tibet and her trek around the sacred mountain. But we can still experience a spiritual peace within the context of whatever religious practice we follow. As a Catholic, raised with the notion of the intercession of the saints—the belief that the saints can pray, or intercede, to God on our behalf—I am comfortable with asking my mother to pray for me. I believe that, united with God, my mother can love me in a way that she—or any other human, for that matter—could not while on earth.

We may find solace and comfort in prayer, remembering Jesus' words in the Bible when he comforted the criminal who was crucified alongside him: "Today, you will be with me in Paradise." In meditation, we may feel ourselves bathed in the white light of eternity, experiencing a union with the Universe, the Source or our Higher Power that unites us all. We may embrace the Zen concept that while we inhabit individual bodies, there is truly no separation between us. To be in touch with ourselves is to be connected with our mothers and all those around us. Whatever our religious philosophy or belief, we can experience a spiritual connectedness at our core, leading us gently on the Path of Understanding to know our mothers—and ourselves.

Many women believe their deceased mothers
have acted like angels, protecting them from harm and
delivering them from serious illness and danger.

There are times when this sense of connectedness feels more tangible, and the spiritual help we receive becomes more immediate. Many of us believe in angels, guardians who watch over and protect us, sometimes intervening directly in our lives to keep us from harm. Other times, those angels appear to be nowhere around when we are hurt physically or endure some grave emotional pain. Or perhaps they provide the strength to endure the hardships. We will never know for sure until we join them. And there are others who believe their mothers have acted as angels, guarding and guiding them out of harm's way.

✣

That is what Susan, a communications executive in Virginia, believes. Her mother died in 1985 at the age of eighty-six, from congestive heart failure. "I needed to say good-bye and let her go," Susan says of her mother's death. But their relationship did not end there.

While preparing for the funeral, Susan and her husband went into one of her mother's closets to pick out an outfit for burial. "I picked out a dress that I knew she liked a lot. I was turning toward the bed away from the closet when I heard my mother's voice say, 'Don't forget my sweater.' My husband and I looked at each other. He had heard it, too," Susan says.

Her mother's sweater was her trademark, a piece of clothing she always carried or wore. "It could be eighty degrees and Mother would say, 'I'm a little chilly. Somebody get me my sweater,'" Susan recalls.

Then in May 1995, Susan faced her own mortality. She was diagnosed with cancer, with two advanced primary conditions in the breast and ovaries. Susan turned to her cousin, Ginny, who is as close to her as a sister. In her anger and concern, Ginny stood in her kitchen, turned her eyes toward the ceiling and screamed "No!" at the top of her lungs. "She looked up—we always think of heaven as being up—and said to my mother, 'Don't let this happen! Do something, goddamnit!'" Susan relates.

Ginny had a sense of being heard and she called Susan to tell her not to worry. "I laughed," Susan explains. "I really didn't overreact to it. I was dubious."

But friends began praying for Susan, and things began to happen. Within a few days, she was in the care of a top doctor at Johns Hopkins University Hospital and, a day or so later, admitted into an experimental cancer treatment program sponsored by the National Cancer Institute. Susan was cured.

The miracle was more than the medicine. It was the timing of being seen by a top specialist in a matter of a few days and then being admitted into an experimental drug program. It couldn't have happened, Susan believes, without her mother. "My mother is a presence that is always with me."

Stories of hope allow us to see possibility of the miraculous in our lives.

It is impossible to explain why some women have experiences such as Susan's, while others do not. In the same vein, we cannot rationalize why some are cured by a means that appears miraculous, while others are not. Whether or not we share the same kinds of experiences, each story offers the power of hope and the possibility of the miraculous in our own lives. Moreover, it seems we cannot demand to have these experiences; mother dreams and visitations do not happen at our command. For most of us, these experiences are gifts from the other side, with a timing so random and yet so perfect that they take on the air of the miraculous.

An Act of Faith, a Leap of Hope

So how do we go about inviting a miracle into our lives? What invitation can we extend to have our mothers appear at our sides? Surely there are meditations and spiritual exercises that put us in touch with a greater Whole outside of ourselves. But few of us, I suspect, walk that path. We are tied up in our own lives; immersed in the earthly with little time to contemplate the heavenly. But we can, perhaps, engender a sense of wonder and the miraculous by opening ourselves to the possibility of a deeper connection.

In prayer and meditation we get in touch with our inner selves, looking for a connection with Infinity.

How we go about that will depend largely on our own religious and philosophic beliefs. We may use prayer or meditation to contemplate what we believe exists beyond ourselves. We may seek the quiet of a church or temple, or the hush of a forest, as we travel inward. We leave our earthly concerns behind for a moment to ponder heaven and our beliefs of what exists beyond this realm. It is not so much an intellectual issue as a spiritual one. We pray, we meditate, we get in touch with our inner selves, looking for a connection with Infinity.

My own experience of my mother followed a prayer of sort, an honest plea for help that went beyond my mind and ego. The answer was the image of my mother, who has been dead since 1986. "Seeing" my mother did not appear "spooky" or "other-worldly" at the time; it seemed like a natural course of events. I have had many dreams of my mother since her death. One or two, perhaps, left me with the feeling upon awakening that she was just there at my side, talking with me. Others have been dreams of the usual variety, as I rehashed and relived the themes of my life.

But nothing could compare with an experience that happened, perhaps a week before I began writing this chapter. That in itself is a bit uncanny, as has been much of the development of this book. Just when I needed a story or a piece of information, it would surface. But this particular experience went far beyond research.

I did not conjure up my mother because I wanted to write about the experience. In fact, I had fully intended to write about something else—an insightful dream I had had shortly after my mother died. But after this experience, I knew I had to write about it.

It was the end of an exhausting and disappointing day. I felt drained, emotionally and physically. On my own as a freelance business writer, I had been at my desk for eighteen hours, finishing up a rush project that I began at the ridiculous hour of three in the morning. It was only nine at night, but it felt as though I had been up for two days. Making matters worse, I was beginning to have doubts, as all writers do, about my writing. I didn't have the emotional, physical or psychological courage to shrug them off, knowing that the right publisher would come my way soon.

As I put my son's toys away, kicking myself that he still wasn't in bed yet, I spoke to my mother out loud. "I'm not so sure I can get this book published, Mother," I said quietly. "I'm afraid I've let you down. If you can do something on your end, I'd appreciate it."

I changed into my pajamas, brushed my teeth, put my son to bed and did not think anymore about what I had said to my mother. As I lay in bed, I suddenly saw my mother. I did not perceive her to be hovering "out there" in the room. Rather, it was as if her image was projected onto my retinas. I thought, "Huh, there's Mother," and the image dissolved. I quieted my mind, and it came back, clearly. I saw my mother in a dirndl skirt and peasant-style blouse, a rather odd outfit that I must say I would not have imagined her wearing. Her short salt-and-pepper hair was pulled back at the sides, and a flower was tucked into the curls behind her ear. She did not look comedic, but rather festive and beautiful.

I focused on this image in my eyes, drawn to the look on her face. She had a sweet expression, very relaxed and happy. She smiled warmly, but without her usual flash of teeth. It was a gentle, knowing smile as her face appeared to be focused on mine. She did not say a word, but gave off a feeling of peace and serenity. Then the image was gone. Exhausted, I rolled over and went to sleep.

I did not know what to make of that experience the next morning when, after eight or nine hours of sleep, I felt like a human being again. But I did know two things: It had not been a dream, and I had not made it up. I saw my mother that night, looking at me with such peaceful surrender that I could no longer worry about my book or my fear of letting her down. With her presence, she had conveyed that to me.

I could try to convince myself that my exhausted mind had conjured up the experience on its own. But I know I was not asleep because after the image faded the first time, I touched my face to confirm that my eyes were open. I could accept the theory that it was a psychological response to my own disap-pointment; that the image of my mother was pulled out of some synaptic archive and presented to me by my own mind. Or I could entertain the prospect that I had somehow "seen" my mother for a few seconds. I cannot will the same image to appear in my eyes, although I can remember what I saw. I am left with the memory of the experience, and the peaceful feel-ing that accompanied it.

(My publisher, by the way, called two weeks after I saw my mother and enthusiastically accepted this book. As I thanked God for this blessing, I prayerfully acknowledged my mother's intercession as well.)

The spiritual experiences we have may leave us hungry for more. But for most of us, these experiences are only glimpses of what appears to exist in another realm. Perhaps that is best. If we were to dwell exclusively in the spiritual realm, we would quickly leave this world. That is, after all, the choice that is made by religious hermits who shun all earthly trappings to focus on the hereafter. But such a calling is undoubtedly a gift that few of us would be able to sustain.

For most of us, spiritual connections are fleeting, a momentary reminder that we are not alone and that what we experience now is not all there is. Then our daily lives call to us: work, home, family, children, pursuits. Yet we go back to the daily grind a little different than before. At the back of our otherwise occupied minds is a memory of something that reached out from beyond us, an experience that even in retrospect is hard to shrug off or explain away. We are left with the unshakable belief that heaven reached down to earth, and that for just a moment, the two realms connected.

Connections

We live our lives at the speed of light. Jobs, responsibilities, ambitions and fears drive us hard, consuming our energy and occupying our minds. Even when we rest our bodies, our minds keep racing. We hash over the events of the day, obsessing about some problem or conflict, and fret needlessly about what might happen tomorrow. And when we are mentally exhausted, we numb our minds with the inane. We "veg out" in front of the television, not focusing on anything in particular, but mercifully distracted from our mental anxiety. (I know— I've done all those things.) What we lose, however, is a chance to reach beyond the physical to the spiritual. Even if we pray, we are often distracted. What we need—mentally, physically and spiritually—is a moment of quiet and meditation.

In a Quiet Moment

- Find a quiet place for a moment of peaceful reflection. It may be in a church, temple or other worship space, or in nature. Empty your mind and focus, just for the moment, on your own aliveness. In meditation, we are told, we quiet our conscious minds, emptying them from mental clutter. In that state of openness, we can connect with our spiritual side.

- Take a walk in nature by yourself. Whether you stroll along a beach or through a forest, concentrate first on your surroundings. Do not dwell on the life that you are leaving behind for the moment. Take in the sounds of nature and feel a connectedness with your environment. Allow the calm you feel to lead you into a meditative state.

- If walking in nature is not possible because of physical or other limitations, listening to a recording of natural sounds or contemplative music can also put us in a meditative state.
- Don't demand too much of yourself as you begin meditation. Experience the quiet within yourself, and leave the noise of the busy world for a quieter existence.

We all dream, even if we don't remember our dreams. Often the images and themes are reflections of what occupies our conscious minds. Sometimes the meaning of the dream is very apparent, a solution to a problem or an insight that bubbles up from our unconscious minds. But sometimes we don't pay attention to our dreams. We consider them to be unimportant musings of our sleeping minds. Dreams, however, have the power to instruct and, some believe, connect us to the spiritual world. By making our dreams important, we invite greater insight into our lives from our unconscious minds and our spiritual natures. All we have to do is ask for the insight and be open to receive the answers.

In Dreams

- Before going to sleep, tell yourself that you are open to receiving insightful dreams. Do this every night, particularly if there is a problem or conflict that you are seeking the solution to. Try to go to bed early enough that you can benefit from a full night's sleep.
- In the morning, replay the dreams that you remember. If they are sketchy or do not seem particularly insightful, don't despair. Often our dreams are very subtle, and the meaning is hidden in the smallest details.

- Write down your dreams in your morning journal, or start keeping a special dream journal. There are many books on dream journals and interpretation that may prove to be helpful.

- Pray before going to sleep. Express your gratitude for the day—even if the blessing is that a difficult day has passed! In prayer, ask for spiritual guidance in your dreams.

- Be open to seeing your mother's face in your dreams. Many of us dream about our mothers but discount its importance. If the experience is that of a "normal" dream, look for meanings from your subconscious regarding your connection with your mother. If the dream seems extraordinary or leaves you with the feeling that you have received a visit, do not merely dismiss the idea. Many psychics believe that in dreams, we do connect with a spiritual realm.

Throughout our lives, we are influenced by our mothers. As we know, even after their deaths, our connection with our mothers is ongoing. In chapter 1, we engaged in exercises of a spiritual nature, such as the Mother Walk, to recall our mothers' essence and invite them into our lives. Now as we do the Mother Walk, imagining her in our lives today, we add another dimension. Seek your mother's loving guidance in your life today, knowing that in a place of perfection she can give you help in ways that were not available to her on earth. Begin a dialogue with her in a way that coincides with your own religious and philosophic beliefs.

Beginning the Dialogue

- In meditation or prayer, we open ourselves to our spiritual side. Now we ask for help and guidance. If you follow an organized religion, pray in the fashion that is most comfortable for you. As a Catholic, I am comfortable with the notion of intercessory prayer, believing that those who are with God can pray or intercede on our behalf. If this is not an idea that you embrace, pray in the fashion that best suits you.

- In prayer, we go beyond our own limits. Think of the times when you and your family, for example, joined in prayer for a common concern such as the health of a loved one or deliverance from danger. In the Bible, Jesus stresses the importance of "two or more" being gathered together. Imagine your mother praying with you now, just as she did when she was alive.

- If you believe in angels or are open to the possibility of spiritual guardians, explore that belief in the context of your own religion or philosophy. Many beautiful, inspiring books about angels and accounts of angelic intervention have been published recently.

- In prayer and meditation, express gratitude for the blessings and insights you are receiving. A grateful attitude draws more blessings, as we open ourselves to deeper spiritual connection and insights.

Those we love are never really separated from us by death, whether we embrace a belief in heaven or an afterlife or not. We may believe their spirits or souls live on eternally in union with God, our Higher Power, the Universe, or whatever terms we use. Or we may see the connection as a psychological one, finding those we love in our own memories and in the faces of the loved ones who remain with us on earth.

8

In Her Memory

Because of the life I've lived, I know there is
only one way I can live the life I have left—as a spiritual
odyssey driven by an unbreakable promise, a solemn oath,
a sacred vow to my mother, to my father, to my sisters,
Vivian and Barbara and Jackie, and my best friend,
Claudette; to shine their light, to carry their torch,
to illuminate their spirit in every song
I sing and in every place I go.

—PATTI LABELLE, *DON'T BLOCK THE BLESSINGS*

$\mathcal{W}$e are our mothers' legacies. Regardless of the paths
we walk, our footprints trace back to our mothers,
who gave us our beginning and who, despite shortcomings and
failings, nurtured us into life. We recall them when we put a
brush stroke on a canvas or roast a Thanksgiving turkey, when
we pin the pattern for a new dress on a length of fabric or open

the door to our own store. As I sit here this morning before dawn, writing while my family sleeps, I recall my mother, the early riser who had the first load of laundry in the washing machine before the rest of us even stirred. Each time I sit down to write this book, here is my mother, sitting with her early morning cup of coffee, to keep me company.

This is not to say that we step out of our own skins and don our mothers' identities, like the little girls we once were who loved to play dress-up. We have gone farther than the generations before us and, as it should be, not as far as the generations who will succeed us. But even when our lives are as radically different from our mothers' as the farm is from the city, or the research laboratory from the family kitchen, we acknowledge our beginnings, the roots from which we stem. For many of us, this acknowledgment has become an integral part of our lives. We honor her past in our present.

Others of us have taken an extra step, engaging in deliberate acts to honor our mothers and our connections with them— whether it be tributes to them on a Web page or college scholarships established in their names. These actions not only recall our mothers; they help keep alive our relationships with them.

Honoring Our Ancestors

Honoring those who have come before us is a natural part of many cultures and religions, particularly in Asia. The followers of Confucius believed that honoring one's ancestors was one of the most important tasks for the living to fulfill. Many of us remember our mothers with flowers on their graves around the anniversaries of their deaths or at special holiday times. Or we may remember them in prayer.

Even if we do not follow a religious tradition that includes a ritualized way of honoring and remembering the dead, we have other ways to acknowledge our ancestral pasts. These include displaying family photographs, such as our parents' wedding portraits, or being the keeper of the family Bible. Gestures we may have taken for granted in the past take on more importance now. The black-and-white snapshot of us as children with our mothers is more than just an object; it is a visual signpost from our past.

We are propelled forward along the road
that was not open to our mothers. We became what
they could not, grateful for their selflessness,
direction and uncommon belief in us.

Even when the relationship has been a difficult one, we cannot forget our past. And when the relationship has been a positive and nurturing one, we would never want to try. Often our mothers propelled us forward, encouraging us to take the road that was not open to them. We became the doctors and scientists that they dreamed of being; we have the financial security and independence that eluded them. Examining our own lives today, we are grateful for their selflessness, direction and uncommon belief in us.

A Mother's Gift, a Daughter's Legacy

Maida's mother came to New York from the Dominican Republic as a young woman, after divorcing her first husband, who was an older and powerful man. She married again and had two daughters, then divorced a second time. It was the 1950s, when single mothers were often viewed with pity if not outright disdain. Maida's mother worked in the garment industry to support her children.

"My mother was a seamstress, and there really wasn't anything she wouldn't do for her family," recalls Maida, who like her sister has been bilingual in Spanish and English since the age of two. "My mother was very creative. She could design things."

Sewing for her daughters or for close friends was a joy for Maida's mother. But the one thing she refused to do was to teach her own daughters how to sew. "She didn't even want us to think about that," Maida says. Her mother had other aspirations for her daughters.

"She told us that she could not give us a fortune or jewels because she didn't have them. But she used to tell us, 'I can give you a good education,'" says Maida, a very successful advertising executive in her forties. Her mother lived to see both her daughters begin successful careers.

And so her mother worked, even after she married a third time to a man whom Maida loved like a father. She sent her daughters to the best schools she could afford, and then to college. She gave them a start in life that she had not had. But she gave with joy and not resentment. "She wanted the best for us," Maida says.

With the financial resources that her mother never had but always wished for her daughters, Maida created a scholarship at her alma mater, Barnard College, in her mother's name. But the legacy does not end there. For Maida there is a strong connection with her mother even nineteen years after her death. "I think of her constantly. I know she's with me every day."

Our lives are not a debt to be paid.
What we do and who we are flows
out of our sense of self.

Our everyday lives recall our mothers each time we create a meal or a work of art. But we do not write or teach or plant a garden out of indebtedness. We have no obligation to repay the love and care we received, no mission to accomplish what our mothers could not. What we do and who we are flows from our sense of self. Whatever we create, whether it's a meat loaf or a symphony, stems from our mission in life and not someone else's. But when we have a chance to be part of something magnificent, to produce the painting or the poem that breaks through our internal barriers and brings us to a new level, we remember the one who bought us the finger paints or taught us our ABC's. When we receive the much-deserved promotion or the standing ovation for our one-woman show, we recall the woman who applauded in the front row of the grade-school auditorium or who adjusted the tassel of our graduation mortarboard cap and said, "I knew you could do it."

We celebrate our gifts and exercise our talents because they were given to us. And in a salute to genetics, sometimes our mothers are creating right along with us. That is what Lawanna feels each time she sings.

❧

"My mother was a singer. Every Sunday in church she was singing," Lawanna recalls, her own speaking voice reflecting the strength and beauty of a gospel singer.

And now, each Sunday, it is Lawanna who sings in church, the soloist who moves the congregation. When she sings, the connection with her mother is so strong, it is as if two voices are blending. "One time when I was singing, one of the women in the church came up to me afterwards and said, 'You sound so much like your mother,'" Lawanna remembers. "And I said, 'That was my mother singing.'"

The talent, of course, belongs to Lawanna. But exercising that talent recalls the woman from whom she inherited the gift, and received so much more. Lawanna's legacy from her mother includes a deep, abiding faith, strong values and a sense of family. "One of my mother's favorite sayings was, 'Be still and know,'" Lawanna recalls. In stillness, we know who we are, where we come from and the love of God that sustains us.

Honoring our mothers cements our connections with them. We find some part of them within us—a talent for singing, an interest in world history and politics—and acknowledge it. We say to ourselves and the world, "This is the woman who was my mother. This is the woman who is her daughter." But honoring our mothers does not plant us back in the past as perennial children hiding in our mothers' skirts. Only as adults can we honor our mothers and take our place beside them.

The Quilt of Life

Together we are like a quilt,
a progression of individual squares that reveal
an intricate pattern. But each square is a
creation in and of itself.

We are part of a progression, one life following the other, each only a blink of the eye of God, and yet special on its own. We are part of a greater whole, and yet unique to ourselves. Enlightened and self-actualized, we learn from the mistakes of our mothers and draw on the strength of their characters. In that, our lives lay down a foundation for those who will follow us, whether they are our own children, stepchildren, or nieces and nephews. Together we are all like a quilt, stitched together in a progression that reveals an intricate pattern. But each individual square is a creation in and of itself, the fabric carefully chosen and the stitches neatly done.

No one knows that better than fabric artist Nancy LeGendre, who helped design and complete the Ovarian Cancer Survivors' Quilt. The quilt was conceived by cancer survivor Shirlee Mohiuddin as a symbol of love and comfort for other women battling the disease. Shirlee posted a request for quilt squares in a newsletter and on the Internet. Many women responded, among them Nancy LeGendre, who lost her mother to ovarian cancer in 1976.

"I decided that I could contribute a square in my mother's memory," says Nancy.

But Nancy's contribution to the quilt became much more than just one square. Shirlee had begun to piece the quilt together, choosing the order of the squares, but needed help. Nancy stepped up to the job. And like each woman who made a square, she also contributed a story. Hers was of her mother, Alice Petteruti LeGendre, "a woman of strong convictions and high ideals."

The daughter of immigrant Italian parents, her mother completed college with honors and a degree in medical technology, establishing a legacy of education that is reflected in Nancy's doctorate in science. Her mother, Alice, married and raised seven children, the sixth of whom was Nancy. Nancy honors the care and nurturing she received in the mothering of her own two children, both of whom have special needs. "My mother was a fierce protector of her brood," Nancy recalls. "She and my father made certain that each of us had the opportunity to pursue our own dreams. Education against a backdrop of certain family love was primary to that pursuit."

Her quilt square is a pattern called Cathedral Window, a highly organized structure that spoke to Nancy of the repeating cycles from one generation to the next. The square's brilliant blue flashes reflect her mother's fierce spirit, the red her love of Christmas. Fifteen hearts of gold and red decorate the square, one for each grandchild.

A red-and-black molecular design represents cancerous cells dividing out of control. "I completed my square within days of the twentieth anniversary of her death," Nancy says. "It is a gift . . . a collection of gems that I wish to give to her, just as she gave each moment selflessly to me in our shared lifetime."

---

*An artist's inspiration comes from within herself.
In that core, she meets her mother and all
the emotions that accompany her.*

For artists, whether they work in paper, stone, fabric, glass or the written word, inspiration comes from within. In that inner place, the artist also encounters her mother, as she wrestles with and revels in all the memories and emotions that accompany her. Perhaps we who journey inward are most aware of our roots and our legacy, the positive and negative, that spring from our mothers and their mothers before them. Whether the work is autobiographical or a science-fiction fantasy, we are both springboard and reference point. We launch ourselves outward while delving inward. Subconsciously and overtly, our work is about ourselves and about our mothers.

Novelist and essayist Joyce Maynard writes about her life. So it comes as no surprise that, as her mother was dying, Joyce wrote of that, too. For Joyce, it was a way of contemplating her relationship with her mother and dealing with the trauma of her mother's death.

"When you lose a parent, the whole rest of your world shifts, I have discovered, which means: I am having to reconsider not just my relationship with my mother, but my relationships with my sister, my children, my husband and my friends, too. I am having to observe—not without some discomfort—that my family can in fact survive without me. Not only survive, but actually flourish," Joyce wrote in her essay, "Nobody's Daughter Anymore." (See Joyce's Web page at *www.joycemaynard.com*.)

Writing is also one of the places where mother and daughter meet. "My mother was also a writer," Joyce explains. "She wrote voluminously about her own life."

As a poet, Susan meets her mother on the common ground of artistry. With her soaring, beautiful soprano voice, her mother could have had an operatic career But she chose a domestic path as wife and mother.

"She chose to have a family instead of pursuing a music career," says Susan, whose poem in honor of her mother, "Intervals, Progressions," appears in the front of this book. "She only sang in church, or at home. I recently listened to a record that had her voice on it. She was way beyond anybody else."

Susan, a writer, editor and musician, recalled how proud her mother was when one of Susan's poems was published. "She showed it to everybody," Susan laughs, "whether they wanted to read it or not."

And when her mother died, Susan gave her that poem to take with her. "The Puritans often put poems in the grave with their dead. So I put that poem in her pocket for her journey."

A Journey Inward

It never ceases to amuse me that my first book to be published is about my mother. Not just my mother, of course; many, many mothers and daughters are part of this book. But when I dreamed of being a published writer, an aspiration I trace back to the age of five, I never knew that the work to break through first would be so much about my mother. During my rebellious twenties, when I wanted to place as much distance as possible between myself and my mother, I probably would have written a book on the dangers of root worm in cornfields before I contemplated the mother-daughter relationship in print. Now it makes perfect sense to write this book.

I could not fully know, understand and love myself as a woman until I understood my mother from the same perspective. So as a writer, how could I grasp my future before I grappled with my past? This book, of course, is dedicated to my mother, as well as all the mothers and daughters whose lives are shared here. I have written it in her honor, but for myself as well—not seeking glory, but understanding. And the role of the writer, of course, is to instruct as well as entertain. Listen to our stories, we writers say, and learn from us.

The Interactive Legacy

Just as our lives are altered and enhanced by technology, so are our gifts and the venues in which we deliver them. When we create a work, our medium can be a Web page as much as a written one. That is what Brenda has created in honor of her mother, and to instruct others of us as well. I came across her Web page (*www.hiwaay.net/~bparris/*) about her mother who died from Alzheimer's disease, and requested an interview. In keeping with this electronic format, our interview was done via e-mail.

"My mother gave me a gift—my home page—to share our story," Brenda writes. "I think my home page gives a personal touch to the information on the Internet—in sharing all of the emotions of the Alzheimer's caregivers, and the grief that is there at all stages of the loss."

Brenda cared for her mother, who first exhibited symptoms of Alzheimer's when she was in her fifties. "There are people who develop Alzheimer's in their forties. So not only do I want to learn all about my mother, to keep her memories with me, but I want to learn all I can about the disease that took her," says Brenda, who at forty-two knows she is at risk for Alzheimer's. "Not only do I want to share it with others, but also for myself and for my family."

Her home page, which includes pictures and stories about her mother, also helped Brenda to come to know her mother and relate her story. It has been a connection that is more than an interactive one. "Doing a page in memory of my mother seemed the natural thing to do, and the poems and a few pictures of my mother came first in July 1996 (three months after my mother's death), along with links to Alzheimer's resources that I could find at the time," Brenda explains.

Then came more pictures, Brenda's poetry, stories about her mother and additional information about Alzheimer's. "I have learned, as many who visited my Web site have told me, that my mother was a very special lady," Brenda says. "She was that, indeed, and there is so much I think I can learn about her."

We have unique gifts with which to express ourselves and by which we can honor our mothers.

A Choice to Honor

Just as we are not called to do the same things, we do not honor our mothers in the same way. For some it may be as dramatic as a painting or as quiet as a candle lit in a cathedral. We remember our mothers on common ground from the kitchen to the studio. If we cook from family recipes, we remember and honor our mother with our culinary creations. In the garden, we cultivate the roses and hoe the sweet peas just as she taught us. Each of us who has stroked the feverish head of a child in the middle of the night recalls our own mothers who came to our bedsides. When we honor our mothers we also acknowledge our own identities and accomplishments. We feel our mothers' pride for us as we celebrate our successes.

How we choose to honor our mothers depends on many things. To begin with, there is the state of our own relationship with her. If conflicts remain, it may be difficult to honor her, and if we do so, it may be out of guilt and resentment. Or we may try to bury her memory along with her physical remains, trying in anger to obliterate every part of her. But the anger and resentment end up being buried deep within us, eating away at our bodies and spirits like a corrosive acid. As discussed earlier in this book, the anger and resentment must be expressed and released. We must free ourselves from the emotional and mental chains that bind us and, more than likely, bound our mother as well.

If our relationships with our mothers were embittered, we honor ourselves—and our mothers— through our efforts to deal with the difficulties.

Even if our relationships with our mothers were embittered, we honor ourselves—and our mothers—by our efforts to deal with and understand the conflicts. We may not think of our trips to the therapist or counselor as a pilgrimage to honor our ancestors, but in fact they are. We honor them by freeing ourselves from their negativity. We release ourselves into health and healing, and in the process cleanse both past and future. By cleanse, I do not mean to whitewash or obliterate. I mean we put an end to the deadly effects of the familial poisons like abuse, alcoholism and co-dependence. The tragic stories remain in our lives, but they become lessons and signposts for how far we have come. We honor our past and our emotional heritage, the sweetness and the sorrows, by owning it as the path we have walked.

In time, we honor our mothers and the women who came before us by deliberately choosing another path. A long line of abusive marriages is broken when we choose healing in our relationships and ourselves. A negative legacy of co-dependent women who feared for their financial security and the safety of their children ends with our ability to take care of ourselves.

We honor our matriarchal ancestors by giving wings and not chains to our daughters. The poison of self-hatred, which caused a mother to lash out at her children or withdraw cruelly from them, is neutralized with self-knowledge and self-love.

❧

Wendy, a writer and poet, wrestles with her relationship with her mother, even ten years after her death. A creative but high-strung woman, her mother had a volatile personality and a hair-trigger temper. "She would be sweet and loving, and then she would snap like that," recalls Wendy.

Her mother's creativity was thwarted by her choice to become a wife and mother instead of the professional singer she could have been. Her outlet was the church and her ambitions for her children. But while her mother encouraged them to pursue higher education and to develop their talents, Wendy believed she pushed too hard.

"I couldn't just sing in the choir; she wanted me to be the soloist," she recalls. "Everything became a difficult task."

Wendy sorts through the complexities and contradictions of her relationship with her mother to make sense of it all. In that, her search for understanding becomes a tribute, of sorts, to her mother and to herself. The understanding enables her to see her mother as she was, an intense and troubled woman who, on her good days, could also be a devoted mother.

Despite the conflict and complexities of their relationship, it is, perhaps, in motherhood and artistry that Wendy and her mother meet. And in these two areas Wendy goes beyond what her mother was able to accomplish, as both a published writer and a mother of two young daughters.

For other daughters, the problem with honoring our mothers is the bitter grief that darkens our view of life and the world. We may be so grief-stricken that we try to lose ourselves in our mothers, trying to become them and to lead the lives they lost. For the Mourners, there is only death and no resurrection of spirit. But following the Path of Understanding enables a Mourner daughter to move beyond that state. The bitter grief subsides, leaving the daughter with a desire to keep a connection with her mother that is nurturing and sustaining.

It is in this time that we may long for a way to honor our mothers' memories. For those of us who are moved to do so, we must first contemplate the ways in which we already have honored them. The lives we lead, the children we raise, the jobs we do are all reflections of who we are and where we have come from. Our life's paths have a beginning, just as they surely will have an end. That beginning is our mother, who—for better or for worse—helped to bring us here.

Motherhood Gratitude List

*We express our gratitude for the positive aspects
of the mothering we received. Acknowledging
the positive, we claim it in our lives.*

On the Path of Understanding, we have come to know our mothers as women. We have contemplated the influences on their lives and how those elements, by extension, affected us. We have seen our mothers through other people's eyes. In chapter 4, which discussed traumatic mother-daughter relationships, we made a list of the positive and negative elements of our early lives. Now with a fuller understanding of our mother and ourselves, we move to the next step on the path, an expression of gratitude for the positive influences our mothers had on our lives.

This acknowledgment, I believe, is a key part of owning our heritage as women. If we do not acknowledge and honor the positive, it remains outside our conscious sphere and we have limited access to it. That, of course, is the basis of the gratitude journals that have become so popular today. Sarah Ban Breathnach in her bestselling *Simple Abundance* encourages readers to make a list every day of at least five things for which we are grateful. By not only counting but listing our blessings, the author believes we attract more abundance into our lives.

"Simplicity, order, harmony, beauty and joy—all the other principles that can transform your life will not blossom and flourish without gratitude," Ms. Breathnach writes.

The same principle of gratitude, I believe, must be used in

our relationships with our mothers. As I contemplate my relationship with my mother—with an understanding of who she was as a woman, and of all the positive and negative influences of her life—I am grateful for many things. As I have said before, my relationship with my mother was not perfect. No relationship between two human beings can be. But there are elements of our relationship that truly blessed me and for which I am truly grateful—my mother's attention to my physical needs, the love she expressed in the service of her family with a clean house and meals on the table. I am grateful for the times she nursed me through childhood illnesses and the fact that she attended every parent-teacher conference and school play (with the exception of one when she had undergone an operation). I am grateful for her religious faith, her love of nature and her joy of cooking Thanksgiving feasts and Christmas dinners.

As each relationship is unique, so will each list be. For some women, the list may be very long. The mothers they experienced were warm, loving, engaged women who were emotionally, physically and mentally able to nurture their children. For others, the list may be shorter, highlighting the care for their physical needs while some of their emotional ones were left wanting. But it is essential that we acknowledge our gratitude for the nurturing we received, even if it is simply the roof over our heads during childhood and warm food to fill our stomachs.

In traumatic mother-daughter relationships, when we were abandoned or abused, one positive can still be acknowledged: A woman bore us and brought us into this world. This does not forgive or excuse any wrongful and damaging behavior inflicted upon us. But it does help us own our right to be here. For even if our mothers so bitterly hated their own lives that they begrudgingly gave birth to us, we could not be here without them. We are grateful for the women who conceived and gave birth to us.

We may choose to expand our list to the other mothers who have had a positive influence on our lives. We recall the contributions to our nurturing from grandmothers, aunts or older sisters. We express gratitude for these influences in order to own them. We integrate the nurturing of the past into our lives today.

Acknowledging and honoring our mothers also empowers us on another level. Since our relationship with them is ongoing, from a psychological and spiritual sense, so, too, are the positive influences. When we honor our mothers for the times they nursed us during illness, we affirm our right to be cared for and to care for ourselves. When we remember our mothers' attendance at our high school graduations, we say that our accomplishments are important. When we acknowledge that without her, we could not be here, we seize our right to be alive.

Connections

We honor the women who came before us, those who gave birth to us and who, to the best of their abilities, nurtured us into life. It begins with an accounting of our relationships with our mothers, an honest assessment of the positive aspects. This gratitude assessment, however extensive or brief it may be, helps us to own the nurturing we once received and to draw it into our lives again. To do this, we begin with a list—however long or brief—of the blessings we gained from our mothers.

The Gratitude List

- Make a list of the aspects of your mother-daughter relationship for which you are grateful. Think of the care and nurturing you received, from homemade soup to hand-knit sweaters. Do you remember being nursed during a bout of chicken pox or the measles? Do you remember your mother baking brownies for the entire third-grade class? Put down everything you can think of, and thank her for what she did for you.

- If your list looks scant because you perceived your mother to be lacking in her mothering, write down whatever you can remember. Even if your mother was emotionally distant or distracted by other family stresses, gratitude for whatever mothering you received will confirm that you deserve love and nurturing.

- If you suffered a traumatic relationship because of your mother's abusive personality, addictions or mental illness, do not fear that your gratitude list will be blank.

Nor will you have to make up a childhood that did not exist. All of us have one important item on our gratitude lists: A woman bore us and brought us into the world.

- Expand your gratitude list to the other mothers of your life. Did your grandmother care for you? Did your older sister teach you how to play the piano? Did your aunt bring you special treats when she traveled?

There are many ways in which we can and do honor our mothers. We do not have to commission a statue or compose a symphony in her memory. Everyday tasks can recall her gifts to us. By undertaking those same tasks in her honor, we foster a deeper connection with her and pass on her loving legacy to the generations that follow. My mother loved family dinners, with everything from bread to dessert lovingly prepared and always homemade. While I do not share her culinary gifts, I remember and honor her flair for cooking and entertaining each time I invite guests for dinner.

In Her Memory

- With a fuller understanding of your mother as a woman, what do you associate her with? Music, art, cooking, church? Find an activity or task that you can accomplish in her honor. What you do can be private, something between only your mother and you, or shared with a circle of intimates.
- Did your mother have a favorite charity or volunteer activity? Did she work with the Girl Scouts or raise money for the American Cancer Society? Find an activity or charitable project that you can undertake in her name. Ask your sisters to join you in the project if the

time and other demands are not too great. (You don't want to turn an innocent project in honor of your mother into a sibling rivalry fest.) Charitable work in your mother's memory can foster a closer tie between you and your sisters.

- Does your father or another relative live in the family home? If so, take care of the garden that your mother left behind, or sort through and dust the china cup collection she loved. Even small acts can be performed in loving memory.

Some of us may be called to a bigger task or a broader project to honor our mothers. What it is will depend on our gifts. But a daughter who has a special gift, including that of financial resources, may choose to undertake a larger project in honor of her mother. Whatever we do should not be acted on out of resentment or a sense of obligation. Resentment taints our efforts and dishonors ourselves. But if we are so moved, there are ways in which we can honor our mothers and exercise our gifts and talents, as the women in this chapter have shown us.

A Special Gift

- What is your special talent—art, music, writing? Consider a work, if you have not already done so, in honor of your mother. Such a creation not only recalls and blesses your mother's contribution to your life but acknowledges the gifts with which you have been endowed.
- If you have the financial resources, you may wish to make a philanthropic contribution or endowment in your mother's memory. If this is within your means and

in line with your intentions, consider a charity or activity that reflects your mother. If she advocated higher education, consider a scholarship or contribution to a school. If she was active in her church or temple, consider a donation to an associated charity.

• If your mother was active in volunteer work, consider supporting her favorite charity in her name, or become involved with it yourself. Charitable organizations often need gifted, committed people to serve on their boards and give time to their special projects. Giving of yourself in honor of your mother is a most meaningful gesture.

Honoring our mothers does not require heroic acts or large sums of money. We can recall and acknowledge their contributions to us and others through even small, anonymous acts. The most important elements are our intentions and attitude. If we give in gratitude and not out of resentment, we truly honor our mothers and acknowledge the women we have become.

9

Celebrating Myself

"All we require—actually, it is quite a lot—
is an initial period of love in a warm climate, where we
feel as one with the person who is dear to us, who is us and we
she, so close it is impossible to know where we begin and she
leaves off. Totally dependent, this symbiosis is heaven. . . .
And yet, and yet, perfect as this heaven is—in part because
it has been so perfect—before the first year of life is over,
we are sated. Enough oneness! Time to push off. Why else
would we leave symbiotic bliss if life's plot wasn't to discover
ourselves, including the unique look of who we are?

— NANCY FRIDAY, *THE POWER OF BEAUTY*

*L*eaving our mothers behind, we step out onto the center of the stage, playing the part for which we were literally made. The spotlight shines on us directly; we share it with no one. Every eye is on us, waiting for the magic we perform, the lines we speak, the music we make. It's our show and we are the only stars.

But wait a minute. Haven't we spent this entire book thus far getting to know our mothers, reconciling with them, bringing them into our lives, honoring them? So why does the focus shift so suddenly? The answer is as simple as the progression of life itself. We leave our mothers for life on our own. We separate in order to become wholly ourselves. Remembering our mothers is a journey. Finding ourselves is the destination.

With a fuller understanding of our mothers and ourselves, we are empowered to move more confidently into our own lives. We will continue to get to know our mothers over time as we age, moving toward and then beyond the ages at which they died. But we also go on our own. It is as it should be.

"For as long as I can remember, I did not want the kind of life that my mother felt she could show me," Nancy Friday writes in the opening pages of My Mother/My Self, first published more than twenty years ago. "Sometimes I think she did not want it either. The older I get, the further away she gets from my childhood, from her ironclad role as my mother—the more interesting woman she becomes. Perhaps she should never have been a mother; certainly she was one too soon. I look at her today, and with all the love and anger in the world, I wish she had had a chance to live another life, mine perhaps. But hers was not an age in which women felt they had a choice."

Choice. It is what separates us the most from our mothers and from the previous generations. We have more choice than they in everything from careers to sexuality. But we pay for that choice with burdens that our mothers and grandmothers could not imagine, balancing sixty-hour weeks and board meetings with preschool pick-ups and junior high basketball games; being a good corporate wife and struggling to keep our identities intact; playing the good provider and the caregiver in a single-parent household. How we handle these choices, our mistakes and our victories, will ultimately become our legacy to the generation that follows. Our sons and daughters will pick over the events of our lives, emulating what they consider to be positive and rejecting the negative—just as we have done with our mothers.

On Our Own

This is the basis of separation. We think of it as an ending, as in the couple who separates as a precursor to getting a divorce. But separation is also a beginning. Just as the infant must separate physically from the mother at birth in order to live, so we must cleave ourselves from our mothers later in life. But separation is not abandonment by either party. It is to stand alone, whole, as a separate and complete entity.

*We grasp our own identities, discovering
who we are and what it is we want to be. That is
the ultimate celebration of ourselves.*

With a fuller knowledge of our mothers as women, we understand what has brought us to this point. Now we grasp our own identities, discovering who we are and creating what it is we want to be. We give ourselves the courage and the confidence to go far beyond what our mothers could, and perhaps farther than we ever dreamed we would. Experience teaches us that we do not have only until the age of twenty-one to fulfill our dreams. We know that we can find a life—and love—at any age. We are works-in-progress until the day we die.

Consider Connie—wife, mother, grandmother and college student in her fifties who is going for her doctorate. It is the completion of a dream that began when she was a teenager who would easily lose herself in a book. It is a dream delayed by marriage and motherhood, albeit happily. But it is a dream that was never forgotten.

Connie spent ten years overseas with her husband, who worked in the oil industry, then came home to Canada determined to go back to university. "I don't know if it was something that crept up on me or if it was a brainstorm. I really wanted to do it. I wanted to go to school," recalls Connie.

Connie's mother was from a Slavic background, a tradition that Connie honored as a doctoral student in her research into Soviet women in the 1930s. Connie's upbringing was somewhat nontraditional because her parents had separated and her mother, a seamstress, had had to work. So Connie shared the household responsibilities, including cooking, which remains a favorite pastime. After high school, there was no chance for Connie to go on to university; she had to get a job with training, and for that reason she had entered the data processing field.

Connie had no intention of going back to data processing. Her mother, who died in 1982, had left her a bit of money, enough to pay for at least one year's worth of tuition and books. This decision was a departure from the previous pattern of her life. "I was always a starter and never a finisher," Connie says. "I think most people believed that going to university was another thing I was going to do for a while, get bored with, and not carry on."

But Connie's honors degree in history turned into a master's degree. She began to get scholarships. Then she was invited to go to a university in Halifax to get her doctorate. "I spent three years there," Connie recalls. "One year, my husband and I saw very little of each other. He was commuting to Nigeria. I figured out that we spent a total of nine weeks that year together."

Connie recently underwent surgery to remove benign brain tumors that had caused seizures. But nothing can slow her down. She will return to Halifax this summer for a teaching job and to defend her doctorate. "I'll be gone again for three months. The hardest thing now is leaving the grandchildren," says Connie. "But I'm not willing to give up what I've worked so hard for."

Atop the Mountain

We go beyond our mothers' lives. Our worlds are usually bigger than the spheres in which they operated, even if our mothers were doctors or lawyers, artists or interior designers. Things, as they say, have changed. We cannot imagine our mothers at the computer, looking up a recipe for spinach soufflé on the Internet or researching the symptoms of some inexplicable rash or disease. But even as we move beyond their world, eclipsing our mothers, we do not block them out. We may have the center stage, but she who came before us more than likely is in the front-row place of honor . . . or in the wings, applauding.

My mother's approval—oh!
What a prize that was in my life.
Even now I am pleased to think
she would be proud of me.

As I look at my own life, I see clearly that it is my mother's praise that pleased me the most. I was and still am very close to my father. I was a Daddy's girl, the youngest of the family, his namesake in lieu of the son my parents never had. But I always had the sense that, when it came to Dad, all I had to do to be loved was breathe. My mother's nurturing was also a constant in my life, even through the conflicts. But her approval—oh, what a prize that was! When Mom approved of me or what I was doing, that was a moment in the sun. Now I am pleased when I hear my aunts tell me that my mother would be proud of me, and I am so happy to have the support and love of these women. But with this book, the culmination of a journey that has changed my life, I am also proud of myself.

Celebrating ourselves, we feel the heady triumph and relief of the mountain climber. Whew! We made it, we say to ourselves. For a moment, we rest atop the pinnacle and enjoy the view. It is not pure ego that prompts us to give ourselves a pat on the back. It is the conviction to pursue our dreams and reach for our goals, understanding how far we've come.

❧

Mary T., a college professor in Illinois, is the daughter of a minister—and is a very nontraditional minister's wife. "My mother cast her own shadow. I see myself in her, in her model," says Mary, the last of six children, born when her siblings were already in high school or college.

Her mother was a partner in her father's ministry, playing the organ at church and active in various organizations. But there were limits to how involved women could be in the church in those days, a topic of study for Mary, who recalls the waves of feminism that rolled through the Lutheran Church in the 1970s and the rifts created by the ordination of women ministers.

Mary regrets that her mother (who surprised the family at the age of sixty-three by getting a job at a department store in downtown Cleveland) died before Mary entered the doctoral program. But she feels confident that her mother would have applauded her pursuit of a higher degree.

"The big sadness in my mother's life was that she couldn't be educated," Mary explains. Her mother, born in 1904 and the fifth of ten children in the family, had to leave school after the tenth grade to help care for her younger siblings. Perhaps that is why four out of the six siblings in Mary's family have doctoral degrees; they accomplished what their mother could not.

"She wanted to learn from us. She had an insatiable curiosity. She learned to drive when she was sixty-seven. She was the kind of person who saw obstacles and overcame them. She didn't have fear," Mary recalls. "When people describe me, they say the same kinds of things. I love being compared to her in that way. I don't think of myself as a clone. But this whole notion of being a strong woman—I see it in myself, my daughter and in my granddaughter, who is only three. A woman who knows her own mind and has a will of her own—that is my legacy from my mother. That is the one I like to claim."

Having It All

We women today are reinventing our lives and our roles. From motherhood to sexuality, it is all up for review. It is as exhilarating as it is scary. Making it even more confusing— and thrilling—is the fact that there is not just one answer to the question of how we lead our lives. We may be stay-at-home moms or single professionals. Unlike the generations of women who came before us, marriage is no longer a prerequisite for having a sex life, and being a mother no longer shuts us out of a career. It is an exciting time to be alive and to be a woman, but a challenging one as well. While we have more freedom and choices than the women who came before us, most of us do not have fewer responsibilities. We have it *all* . . . and sometimes it seems like too much.

⯏⯏

Amy, a successful professional with her own business and the mother of two children, says the backpack has become the bane of her existence. She's only half joking. Each morning there is the backpack to fill with homework that needed to be checked, permission slips that needed to be signed, lunches and snacks, and clean clothes for sports practice. Each night there is the backpack to unload. "Your children suffer if they are unprepared," she says. When Amy speaks of her children it is obvious she takes her role as their mother to heart.

For Amy, managing a household, caring for two children engaged in a variety of sports and extracurricular activities, and sometimes playing the corporate wife makes for a busy-enough life. Add to that a thriving software business, which has caught the eye of venture capitalists and larger corporations that want to make a deal. Amy has her hands full in a way that her mother could not imagine.

What makes Amy special, and at the same time so symbolic of our age, is the way she views her life. Yes, there is understandable and well-deserved pride for all she has accomplished, including building a business from scratch. But there is the introspective side as she wonders how she will balance it all as she goes forward; what might slip and what might drop. She wonders how her son and daughter view her—especially her daughter, who, Amy feels, longs for her to become a more active parent volunteer at school. In the midst of accomplishments that women a generation ago could not fathom, Amy is looking critically at her life, wanting to make the right decisions for the future.

While the details will differ, Amy's life may look surprisingly like ours if we are also working wives and mothers. We who are childless may not have backpacks to worry about, but chances are our careers are more demanding than our mothers' jobs because the working world has changed so dramatically. And if we are single, we are carving out a life for ourselves that is light years beyond the "career girls" and, God forbid, "old maids" and "spinsters" of previous generations. We don't need a man to define our lives. Married or single, we have learned that our identities are our own and not community property.

We may imagine that our mothers may have been uncomfortable with our life choices as we discard traditional roles. Perhaps we perceive that our mothers would be appalled at the dust on our bookshelves and the take-out food on our dinner tables. Or maybe we feel that way about ourselves. As I survey my desk at this moment, and its clutter of research papers, I remember the cleanliness of my mother's house. When I think about what I ate for dinner last night (vegetables in a plastic pouch that I "nuked" in the microwave and a piece of pre-cooked breaded chicken), I recall the homemade meals she prepared each night. Her freezer was full of food she cooked herself and vegetables from her garden. Shelves in the basement were lined with jams, jellies and preserves made from fruit she picked. In the domestic role, I am a poor comparison with my mother.

---

*We may imagine that our mothers would
not approve of our lives as we discard traditional roles.
But we are the ones who judge us.*

But it is not my mother who sits in judgment of me; I do. As I become more comfortable with my life choices, I am more at peace with myself—and my mother. I know that my calling is not to make strawberry jam and apple butter, at least not at this time in my life. I flip through the pages of *Martha Stewart Living* to amuse myself after a long day of writing, but I know I will never embroider chair covers or make individual soufflés baked in a lemon rind. That is where my mother and I part company. While I feel a closeness to her and find many similarities between us, our lives are dramatically different. Giving myself permission to have that difference, I celebrate my life with the words I have written.

That permission is nothing less than the freedom to live freely and honestly. And as society changes, it is permission that women must give themselves. I recall the words of a woman at a recent workshop I gave on mother-daughter relationships. The question I put to the group was this: How are your daughters' lives different from your lives and your mothers' lives? A woman in her late fifties quickly spoke up.

"I certainly had more choices than my mother had, but there were still boundaries, a framework of what I was supposed to do," she explained. "But young people today have more choices. Even in a marriage, they are both doing their own things. They don't have that framework of what they're supposed to do. I think that can be difficult at times."

Freedom of Choice

Bingo, as they say. Today we do have more freedom of choice. We are encouraged to "do our own thing," which sometimes puts us at odds with our partners, who are similarly pursuing their own "thing." But perhaps it is not our partners' dismay that worries us. Maybe it's not our peers we fear will condemn or judge us. Perhaps we wonder how our mothers would view us and our lives.

"Women don't feel free to make the choice," Nancy Friday says quickly when I tell her this story. "The unconscious part of them says, 'What would Mommy think? Mommy wouldn't let me do that. I can't play that game. I can't wear those clothes. . . .'"

Our freedom to make choices for our own lives, to assume and embrace our own identities, is very much tied to our relationships with our mothers. By growing into a deeper knowledge of her, we learn to appreciate ourselves. We can step into our own shoes and walk the path our way.

To some extent, each of us believes there are things about us that our mothers could not and would not accept or understand. Our sexuality. Our independence. Our career goals. Our decision to leave our husbands. Our desire to go back to school or start our own business. "We think our mothers can't handle the truth about us," says Linda Dillon, a psychic and lecturer in Arizona, whose mother died recently.

We've lived in a stew pot of resentment,
anger and self-loathing, believing that our mothers
would never accept the truth about us.

Believing our mothers wouldn't accept the truth about us, we reject it as well. No wonder so many of us have lived in a stew pot of resentment, anger and self-loathing. But when we grasp who we are and where we've come from, we get out of that simmering pot of negative emotion. And sometimes to our surprise, we find that our mothers would have understood us all along. One of my favorite stories to illustrate this point comes from Linda, my gifted psychic friend.

When Linda became aware of her intuitive nature, she shared her abilities first with a few friends and later with her siblings. But she did not dare tell her mother that she was then a practicing psychic. What, after all, would her mother think? Finally, Linda decided to come clean and to tell her mother about her experiences. "She said, 'That's interesting. You know your grandmother was a psychic,'" Linda recalls, laughing.

At the core of it all, I believe, is our honest desire not to disappoint our mothers. We don't want to let them down; we are, after all, "good" daughters at heart. But then we wrestle with where our mothers leave off and we begin. That is the parent-child struggle that will undoubtedly last for the rest of human history. But outside of the parent-child relationship, as adult women we can find equal ground. We embrace the positive aspects of our mothers and reject the negative. We can love our mothers and still not like—and even hate—certain things about them. We can feel a connection with them, but vow to live differently.

For many of us, the decision to lead lives that are different from our mothers' is born out of survival, if not of necessity. After living with our mothers' illnesses and traumas, from depression to alcoholism, we choose healthier lives. We meditate, exercise, go to Twelve-Step programs, and undergo therapy and counseling, wishing that our tormented mothers had had the same options available to them.

Just as our therapy sessions can honor our past as we unlock the secrets to how our families functioned—or "dysfunctioned"—so, too, they become a celebration of ourselves. We make the choice not to be driven by the same demons that tormented our mothers. As healthier women, we are better able to care for our children, making up many times over for the lack of what we experienced in our lives. We are deservedly proud of the lives we've carved out for ourselves and our families and the healthier choices we've made. We understand what Wendy, a poet and writer who had a traumatic relationship with her mother, means when she says with pride, "I wish my mother could see me. We have a lovely house in the suburbs. I have these absolutely gorgeous kids that I would love for her to see."

Perhaps they do see from a new vantage point. Whether we reconnect with our mothers psychologically, spiritually or both ways, they are ever-present to us. Whether we picture our mothers in heaven, on another spiritual plane or part of the universe around us, perhaps now they can see and, through us, understand. We will not know for sure until we, too, have died, leaving behind a generation that will ponder us and our lives. In the meantime, we have an obligation to our ancestors, our children and, most of all, ourselves. We must live well.

From Daughters to Parents

When we love and accept ourselves, all areas of our lives improve. We become better able to accept and give love in our relationships. We are less emotionally needy in our friendships because we're not looking for everyone else to make up for some lack in our childhood. We're better workers, more confident in taking on new challenges and accepting constructive criticism. And when we acknowledge our faults and frailties and the challenges of our childhoods, we do not become weaker parents, but rather, more empathetic ones.

Healthily separating from our mothers, we allow our children the same freedom. Seeing our mothers as women, we can see our children as individuals, unique and different from us. In fact, it is imperative that we grow into our own lives as adult women who have a fuller understanding of our mothers—not only for ourselves, but for the sake of our children. "If you don't do this work beforehand, it's going to shadow you, when you have your own children," Nancy Friday cautions. "When your little girl becomes a sexual creature, you are going to communicate nonverbally if not verbally the whole message that all the sexual parts of her body smell bad, look bad and Mommy doesn't like it. It's going to be passed on to another generation."

---

*The difference between our lives now and
the context in which we grew up can be disconcerting.
We have to give ourselves permission
to change the paradigm.*

On the Path of Understanding, as we view our mothers as women, we face again their views of love, sexuality and marriage. Our own views on these topics are often so enmeshed with our mothers' opinions that it is difficult to see where their influence ends and our choices begin. We struggle with our mothers' "good-girl" values that raised chastity to a super-human level, while longing for a committed, monogamous relationship. We don't want a fifties marriage or life in the sexual fast lane, either. Many of us live in the world more than our mothers did, with careers and lives outside the home that at times seem in conflict with marriage. But are they? Maybe it's only that our lives are in conflict with the kind of marriage our parents had. In the context of our own time, everything is just fine. But the difference between our lives now and the context in which we grew up can be disconcerting. The base comparison doesn't work, and we have to give ourselves permission, in the parlance of the business gurus, to change the paradigm.

Anita and I chatted at the playground while our sons dug in the sand on an unseasonably warm day in early spring. It was a Friday afternoon, a time I would normally be at the office or at my desk. But with a shift in my professional career to freelance business writer, I had given myself more flexibility. Anita, a nurse, said she had put aside her studying to come to the park. Within the first moments of conversation, we had sized each other up as working mothers. (This is, by the way, one of the more interesting social dances at the playground: watching the mothers line up—mentally, of course—with working mothers on one side and stay-at-home mothers on the other. Neither one is right or wrong; we should not judge another woman for whatever choice she's made.)

Anita and I were discussing marriage. Her mother was also a nurse and had worked all her life, helping her father support the family. Anita says she could give up her part-time nursing job, but she can't bring herself to do that. "I can't do that to my husband," she says gently. "I think it would be such a huge burden on him."

As Anita and so many women know firsthand, it often takes two incomes to support a middle-class lifestyle. Corporate downsizing has made even long-term jobs less secure than in our parents' day. Or we may be the main breadwinner in the family.

For many of our mothers, the ideal was for a woman to marry a good provider who would bring home the paycheck to support the household that she ran. It wasn't better or worse than what many of us have chosen; just different. We may work outside the home, bringing home paychecks that are equal to or greater than our husbands'. Or we may put our careers on hold to raise the children. The key difference, I believe, is our choice in the matter to a greater degree than our mothers had. It is sad, therefore, that we feel a need to defend ourselves in whatever decision we make. We can do ourselves and our sisters of the world a huge favor by stopping the unfair comparisons. We can drop the smugness when we tell the stay-at-home mother about our success at balancing home and career. We can stop the judgment when we tell the working mother how much quality time we have by staying home with our children.

We're all in this together, stumbling along and praying we're not making too many mistakes with our children. Perhaps that is one outgrowth of understanding these women who came before us. When we are more comfortable with them and ourselves, we can stop comparing our lives with everyone else's. We can stop looking for validation and affirmation through comparisons, instead making decisions by what we deem to be best for our particular situation. As women, we must be supportive of each other.

Motherhood: No Panacea

At the center of so many of our lives is the issue of motherhood—our mother's experience of it and our own. And as we move into our own lives, there is the acknowledgment that motherhood is not a panacea. Don't get me wrong: I love being a mother. It is the single best thing I have ever done. But as rewarding as it is to feel Patrick's small hand in mine when we walk together, it is a challenge and a responsibility that I cannot underestimate. The mistakes I will inevitably make will affect him, although I pray not seriously. I will be cranky at times and loving at others; short of temper one day and long on patience the next. But most of all, I will be myself. As Patrick gets older, I pray that he comes to know me as a person. But for the next dozen years or more, I will probably be mostly just a mother to him.

*We ask ourselves, How can we be good mothers
without losing our identity in the process?*

Patrick is a fairly easygoing kid, quite good-natured although as demanding as any young child can be. He wants to play his preschool computer games just when I'm on a roll at the keyboard. He pesters me when I'm on the telephone, taking a business call. But I love this dual life of mine, mother and writer. Without this perspective, I doubt I would have been able to do this book. And on the Path of Understanding, I have come to know something else about myself and, by extension, my mother. It is a question that I believe many women struggle with, especially while their children are young: How can I be a good mother without losing myself in the process?

I remember reading a book, *Your Baby and Child: From Birth to Age Five*, by child-rearing expert Penelope Leach when I was expecting Patrick. This gentle guide to parenthood and babies was written in a soothing, positive tone to give confidence to those of us who were venturing into new territory. Then I read THE LINE, the one that struck terror into my heart. It said, in essence, that given the demands of a baby, it's best to take it easy on ourselves. This is not the time, Dr. Leach advised, to start our new novel. But that was exactly what I was doing: writing seriously and consistently through my pregnancy. And now Dr. Leach was telling me I had to stop!

For the first three months of Patrick's life, I did put my personal writing on hold, even though I had to go back to work when he was six weeks old. I was working full time, still breastfeeding and pumping milk in the bathroom at work, and trying to be a good mother in his waking hours. Then during his sleeping hours, I began to write again. I pushed myself, giving up the naps that would have made me a more rested person, if not a saner one. Even now, I choose to write in the very early hours of the morning—I began at 3:30 A.M. today—not only for the absence of distraction, but also so that I did not have to choose between Patrick and my writing. If it came down to that, I would, of course, choose Patrick. But I've found a way to do both. My solution has been to forgo a lot of sleep, to make friends with the coffee bean and the tea leaf, and to write. I kept both parts of my life essential to me. It was the way I found to stay true to my nature, my identity as a writer, while not sacrificing my motherhood.

A New Perspective on an Old Story

I do not mean to come off as heroic or super-human. Ask anyone close to me and they will tell you I am neither. I'm just a working mother like so many others, juggling it all and hoping I don't drop anything important. In that, my life is so different from my mother's, who devoted herself to home and family. It was the area in which she could distinguish herself, with beautiful flower gardens, an immaculate house and dresses she made for herself and her three daughters. But there is another place where we meet, and an incident that once was hurtful is now enlightening.

My mother's second cousin was coming to visit. A celebrated Canadian poet, Edna Jacques had written several volumes of poetry, a copy of which my mother proudly owned. Now Edna Jacques was coming to visit our grandfather, my mother's father, and Mom was going to have a chance to meet her. But the day she came to visit was the day that I, then seven years old, came down with strep throat—in the middle of summer when the warm weather mocked me and my wintertime illness. Fearful of spreading my germs, my mother stayed home that day, so disappointed she couldn't meet Edna Jacques that I could hear the anger and sadness in her voice.

I felt ashamed and guilty that day because I knew I was the cause of my mother's unhappiness. And I felt righteously indignant because, after all, it was not my fault that I got sick. For years that story was in my arsenal of "mean old Mommy" stories. But now I see that incident in a new light, and I bless my mother for showing her disappointment to me. She wasn't angry at me per se, but at the unfairness of motherhood; the fact that she had to sacrifice something she really wanted to do (and never had a chance to do again, by the way) because of one of her children. I am glad she didn't hide her anger and disappointment, or disguise her voice that was choked with tears when she called Grandpa to say she wasn't coming. She showed me in that incident that she struggled at times with the same issue that I do: how to be a good mother without losing yourself.

I don't have an answer to that one, except to say that I am working every day to be the best parent I can while remaining true to myself. I do not know what complaints my son will have about me when he reaches adulthood; what he will judge as the "bad" things I did and the "good" ones. I hope he always knows how much I love him, beyond the words that I say so frequently. I hope he understands why I write so much, that it is so much a part of the woman I am. And I hope he knows why I choose to write in the middle of the night or at times when he is otherwise occupied. I hope he sees that I tried to balance his needs and mine.

We do the best we can, balancing
our needs with the needs of those around us.
We cannot deny our needs as our mothers did,
to their detriment and ours.

That is the best we can do, in the long run. We balance our needs with the needs of those around us—not deny them, as so many of our mothers did, to their detriment and ours. Celebrating myself for the woman I am, I honestly acknowledge what I need.

As we reach this juncture on the Path of Understanding, our challenge is to view ourselves in the same light that we examined our mothers' lives. We see where the mother ends and the woman begins. We allow ourselves to be sexy, desirable women, independent and yet able to be fully committed partners. We allow ourselves to have our own opinions and our own checkbooks, our triumphs and our failings. We accept ourselves and our bodies throughout the stages of our lives. A stone's throw from age forty, I am growing more into myself. I still swallow hard at the thought of leaving my thirties in less than one year. But I know that dreams can be pursued at any age, that love doesn't grow old, and that most of the limitations we face are in our own minds.

Aging as a Positive

At each stage of life, there is opportunity and possibility. Our society continues to worship at the altar of youth, but we must not turn our backs to those who are older and wiser . . . especially when we are in those ranks! We may long for a firm body and a wrinkle-free face, but we cannot hide the marks of experience. We have earned every gray hair and every wrinkle. To honor ourselves is to wear our age proudly; we celebrate our lives, acknowledging the past and looking forward to the future.

"I just turned seventy. I'm delighted to be seventy," says Marge, an author and retired teacher and administrator in Wisconsin. "I have this thing that if we don't brag about our age, it turns into a negative."

With her attitude, it's not surprising that Marge's doctoral dissertation was on creativity in aging women, born out of the art and design courses she began taking when she was in her forties. Marge's life now is an evolution from where she began, including the high school girl who contemplated her future and decided to become a minister's wife. "I thought, who gets recognition in this world? At that time, I thought it was clergy. I had grown up in the church so I thought I would marry a clergyman."

She met her husband, Ken—a clergyman—and married him. Luckily for Marge, her husband and her marriage grew along with her as she became a rather staunch feminist. "I did the clergy-wife thing, which was a heavy role, almost like being an associate minister. Then I got just really bored to tears," Marge recalls. She moved out of the clergy-wife role with the support of her husband, despite the fact that the wife of a particular bishop told Marge she was jeopardizing her husband's career.

Now she looks back on her life only to sort out her past, including her relationship with her parents. She recounts an incident in which she and her mother discussed her father, whom Marge feels disapproved of her much of the time. "I told my mother that I didn't think she was always very supportive either," Marge recalls. "She looked at me and said, 'I had to think like he thought.' I just about flipped. That opened all sorts of doors to me. I couldn't imagine having to do that—to think the way my husband did."

But Marge's focus is not on the past. Regardless of one's age, she believes in looking ahead and being open to new experiences. "The brain research is very exciting. An older person's brain can be just as alert as a younger person's brain," she says. Marge intends to prove that.

*We are part of a progression,
called to move forward with our lives.
That is what we celebrate.*

Whatever age we are, whatever the circumstances of our lives, we must accept ourselves. Like most women, I would love the opportunity to rewrite many chapters of my life, but that, thankfully, is impossible. As much as we'd like to right the wrongs that we inflicted and that were inflicted upon us, rewriting the past would keep our focus there on the years behind us. But we are part of a progression, called to move forward. That is what we celebrate.

We don't need a Nobel Prize or a blue ribbon from the county fair, for that matter, to celebrate our lives. The only requirement is self-acceptance. What a hard-fought battle it is to attain that prize. And for most of us, the contest never ends. We judge ourselves and everyone around us, not because we are hypercritical, but because we are insecure in who we are. Life is a continual evaluation of choices, some we deem to be good and others we later decide were bad. But the only mistake we can ever really make is the failure to see who we are. Self-negation serves no purpose. It is death, long before we stop breathing.

Instead, with the full knowledge of all the mistakes, wrong turns, bad choices, failed relationships, lost opportunities, triumphs, rewards, luck and hard-earned victories of our lives, we accept our right to be. That is what we celebrate, simply by being ourselves.

The Map Maker

Few of us actually chart the progress of our lives. We should take the time to look back and view the events of our lives in a linear fashion. Plotting the points as if on a graph, we can see the highs and lows.

Charting the major events of my own life, I see the depths and heights of the past fifteen years. (I chose fifteen years because, at thirty-eight, it allowed me to reflect back to when I was twenty-three. Any time frame of ten years or more will give the same perspective.) But each point of the chart reveals something about my journey thus far. Looking at even a rough depiction of it, I see clearly how far I've come. On another piece of paper, I chart a future course. Like a cartographer, I plot the lay of the land ahead of me as I hope it will be. I see a steady rising slope connecting the dots of my hopes and dreams. The line arches as it rises higher and higher.

I look back at the journey behind me, seeing the peaks and valleys. My future, however, I have plotted to look like the upward arch of an ever-rising rainbow. Chances are, if past performance is any indication of the future, there will be valleys ahead of me as well as peaks. Where will they occur, I wonder, looking at the charted course of my dreams. How far down will I dip; how high will I rise? Regardless, I know I will survive the downturns in the future as I have in the past.

We are often stronger than we realize and braver than we give ourselves credit for being. The past gives us courage for the present. That is ultimately how we celebrate ourselves, by honestly assessing how far we've come and plotting where we someday hope to be.

The Celebration

Look at the map of your life, the highs and lows of the journey you've made thus far, and scan the horizon of your dreams. That is worth celebrating. It doesn't matter how many lost jobs and failed marriages are on that life map, or if there are more question marks than goals on your future course.

Life is worth celebrating. Literally. We don't take time to acknowledge ourselves. The best parties we throw are for other people. We hide our age and therefore duck our birthdays. We say we'll buy a new dress when we lose that ten pounds we've carried for the better part of ten years. When do we get to celebrate us—when there is a new "us" to take over? No. For one thing, there is nothing wrong with who we are now. And whatever plans, changes, dreams and goals we have for the future, we'll give ourselves a better chance of achieving them by simply accepting where we are today. Maybe where we are is no longer comfortable. Perhaps we've outgrown our circumstances, or we've found the courage to give up an addiction. We're headed into therapy or back to school. Celebrate right where you are—your life now and the course you're embarking on.

If all this celebration of yourself seems too selfish or narcissistic, do it privately. Be thankful for life thus far. Make a pilgrimage to a place you consider sacred or meditative, whether it's a cathedral or a sculpture garden. Know that, whatever your journey, you've come a long way.

But consider a broader celebration. Can you think of throwing a party just because you have some fabulous friendships that you want to honor? Can you buy yourself flowers just because it's Tuesday? Can you imagine taking off a day for a session at the spa, a trip to the hairdresser and manicurist, a walk at the nature center? Can you give yourself an hour in the middle of a busy weekend to just sit in the backyard or in the park and feel the sun on your face? Can you go to Rome simply because you've never seen the Coliseum before? Can you try the new Thai restaurant in town because you've never eaten that kind of food?

Whatever you do, from a cup of tea to a Caribbean cruise, do it in celebration of yourself. Acknowledge who and what you are with love and acceptance. You know where you've come from, and you understand the woman who figured so prominently in your life. Now it's time to move into the rest of your life, whether your future is measured in months, years or decades. Embrace time; it is a gift.

It is early morning now, and the world is just waking up. The spring birds are making quite a racket outside, and by the fence the tulips are beginning to bloom. Inside my home, my husband and my son are still asleep but will be stirring soon. I savor the last hour of solitude at my desk. As I write, I see on my office wall the portraits of my past—my grandfather's watercolor of an old mill, my parents' wedding picture, a black-and-white photo of my father with his parents and six siblings that was taken in the 1950s, my father holding my son as a baby, Patrick as a three-year-old, and, of course, the photo that started it all: my mother in her strapless gold brocade dress, standing in a chorus line of women. I treasure that photo for the spirit of her that it captured, laughing and beautiful. But she was more than just a lovely object to look at. She was a real woman, a wife, a mother, a sister, a daughter and more.

I have come to know her well over the past year. I feel her presence in my life and in my memories.

I see another picture on my wall, a recent snapshot taken at Patrick's preschool. In it, I'm reading a storybook to Patrick's class while he sits beside me. I laugh at my leggings and belted shirt, the little black boots and my wild-looking hair. It's not the mother uniform that I grew up with, but it's my style. My mother used to go to parents' days at my school, just as I attend Patrick's. But I go my own way. It is, after all, the way it's supposed to be.

Connections

We are our own women, the products of our pasts and our life choices. We may see more similarities than differences between our lives and our mothers', or we may see exactly the opposite. Whatever life we're living, it is ours. The journey of this book has been to get to know our mothers again, to feel a connection with them in our lives as a means to understand them from a new perspective—that of the women who came before us. We've vented our feelings, researched her past, talked to her peers and constructed a portrait of this woman who was our mother. We understand her. But we don't end there. Our destination is ourselves. We step to the center of the stage, into the spotlight, acknowledging our own lives.

Life on Your Own

- How is your life similar to your mother's? Do you share the same interests? Do you have similar occupations? Did you both stay home to raise your children? Are you both single parents?

- How is your life different from your mother's? Are you more independent and financially secure? Do you have a career? Have you chosen to remain single? How do you feel about those differences? Can you feel a connection with your mother in spite of a lifestyle that is the polar opposite to hers?

- What is it about yourself that you like the most? Your compassion, intelligence, talent? Be honest with yourself. Write down a list of ten terrific things about you. No one but you will see the list, so don't be shy. Now read over your list and put down ten more things. Acknowledge your smile and your singing voice, your ability in math and your religious faith. Write it all down.

- What is it about yourself that you don't like? Your temper, your jealousy of other people? Write down a list of five things that you would like to improve. Don't exercise enough? Put that down. Need to work less and play more? Note that one too. But list only five things. Our perception of what is "wrong" with us is often skewed by a false image of ourselves that is neither loving nor nurturing.

- Look at both lists. Can you accept being a funny, intelligent, loving woman with great legs, a warm smile and high energy, who sometimes loses her temper, should eat more green vegetables and drinks too much coffee? Is it okay to be a compassionate, friendly woman with deep religious faith, a hard worker and a good cook, who gets irritated by small things easily and bites her nails? The answer is yes, whatever your list reveals. You are perfectly wonderful just the way you are. We can't reach our goals without loving ourselves just the way we are today.

No one has lived a perfect or charmed life. We see the woman in town who appears to have it all—the looks, the house, the husband, the kids, the car. She dashes across the street and looks like a perfume ad. She shows up at the playground in jeans and a sweatshirt and looks like she's on the fashion runway. I've got news for you: She's not as perfect as she seems. Not that we want to build ourselves up by tearing other people down. But we all live with these comparisons that someone else has it all together while we're still fumbling around in the dark. The truth is, we all fumble around in the dark sometimes. To find our way, we need to turn on the light of understanding and take a look at the map of our lives. We chart where we've come so far, and we plot a course for the future.

The Map Maker

- Take a legal-size sheet of paper and turn it sideways so that the length of it runs across your desk or table. Starting at the far left, put a small X in the middle of the page and mark it "My birth." Continuing along the page, mark the significant points of your life, putting the X's as either high or low points, depending on how you felt at the time. If one sheet of legal paper isn't enough, tape two or three together. Now connect the X's and look at the peaks and valleys of your journey thus far.

- Taking another legal-size sheet of paper, plot the course of the future. What would you like to do or achieve in the next several years? Travel, have a child, change jobs, retire? Mark those X's along the course, mostly likely as a string of high points. (I know low points in our lives are inevitable, but let's not make them our goals.)

- Now compare the two maps. If past performance is any indication of the future, there will likely be peaks and valleys ahead just as there were behind you—although perhaps not as many valleys going forward, and many more peaks. By looking at the future in light of the past, we see we have the courage to endure whatever down-turn might come our way, and that we are braver than we think. We also have the ability to embrace the high points without losing perspective or getting scared.

If your best friend received a promotion, would you take her out for lunch? If your sister decided to go back to school, would you throw her a graduation party? If your cousin left an abusive relationship, would you send her flowers? If your daughter was feeling blue, would you buy her a card to tell her how wonderful she really is? Of course you would. Now, pretend that you are that friend, that sister, that cousin and that daughter, and celebrate yourself.

We may not be comfortable with this idea. After all, remember those five negative things about ourselves that we listed? We can't possibly celebrate ourselves until there's nothing on that list (and that list could be a lot longer). Besides, we haven't accomplished anything really. Our lives are certainly not that special. There is no reason to celebrate. . . .

Wrong. Whatever life we have, whatever choices we've made, whatever relationship we're in or not in, we have a reason to celebrate. The first step is simply to accept who we are, proverbial warts and all. The next step is to make a little ritual out of it because the more we embrace who we are, the more we allow ourselves to move forward. And that is definitely worth celebrating.

Rituals, Parties and Celebrations!

- What would you most like to do for yourself that is within your means and the realm of possibility? A weekend trip, a day at the spa, lunch with a friend at a new restaurant? A cruise? A party?

- Don't look for an excuse to treat yourself to your celebration. Don't wait until it's your birthday or you get that raise. Maybe you'll need some time to plan that dinner party for ten that you've wanted to throw just for the heck of it. But plan it just for the sake of celebrating your life.

- Quiet, private celebrations are extremely meaningful and help to keep the focus on ourselves. Treat yourself to some meditation time in a place you consider to be sacred or restorative. Sit in the backyard or the park, and feel the sun on your face and the breeze on your skin. Be grateful for being alive.

- Love yourself, exactly as you are. There is no one quite like you.

Epilogue

Into the Future

It is through love that we elevate ourselves.
And it is through love for others that we assist others to
elevate themselves. Love, the extension of the self, is the
very act of evolution. It is evolution in progress.

—M. Scott Peck, *The Road Less Traveled*

"Where is Grammy now?" my son, Patrick, asked me one day.

His question was a natural one, since I had been telling him a few things about his grandmother to make her more real to him. I told him how his Grammy, as Patrick refers to her, loved to ride a bicycle, swim, walk in the woods and play in the snow in the wintertime. These are all activities that Patrick enjoys and, frankly, they are things that I like as well. But then he wanted to know where she was.

It was a moment of truth for me, as it is for a lot of us. The Path of Understanding asks us to ponder issues that, until recently, our culture has tried to avoid: mortality, our concept of the afterlife, religious and philosophical beliefs.

Our mothers are within us, around us and beside us. We find reminders of their love and nurturing in friends, lovers and spouses. We find their gentle touches in the way we treat our own children. They are beyond us, in the next life, in heaven and part of the universe.

Where are our mothers now? The question is intensely personal, as are the answers. When Patrick asked me, I gave him the answer that is Truth as I see it.

"Grammy is dead. She is in heaven," I said. "She lives with Jesus. And she loves you very, very much." I pointed to the sky for effect, even though I do not think of heaven as a place but rather a spiritual state of being.

The answer seemed to suffice for the moment as Patrick, who at the time was not quite four, got on his blue tricycle for the ride home from the park. I walked along beside him, carrying sand shovels, a bucket, and a fleet of toy trucks and bulldozers.

I feel my mother's presence in times like these, knowing how much she would enjoy playing with Patrick. But it goes beyond just imagining her beside him at the sandbox, digging holes and building castles. I feel her presence in my relationship with Patrick. The mothering I received is mothering that I can give. The healing I experienced as my mother's daughter has spread to all parts of my life.

A Fundamental Shift

I still have my moments of anger, frustration and insecurity. But there has been a fundamental shift in my life. I no longer look for my husband, my friends or my son to make up for some deep loss in my life. I experience love and nurturing from them, but they do not have to "pay" for some long-ago hurt or deeply ingrained resentment.

That is the real power of the Path of Understanding. The journey to know our mothers as women leads to a fuller acceptance and love of ourselves. But it does not end there. It continues on, into the future, toward the next generation.

By reconnecting with our mothers, finding solace, comfort, understanding and forgiveness, we open ourselves to a deep healing. As a parent or someone who is involved in the lives of children, the healing flows from us to the next generation. We break the chains of negativity that span generation to generation, behaviors that had seemed so ingrained in us they were nearly unconscious.

Aware of the pain we felt when our mothers criticized us— out of their own poor self-image or good intentions gone awry—we make a conscious decision not to do that to our children. Remembering how soul-deflating it was to hear that we couldn't try something (our mothers' desire to protect us from risk), we give our children encouragement. Knowing how we needed love to be expressed verbally and physically when we were children, we give that to our own families.

The journey of remembering mother and finding myself brought me home and set me free. I left a place of motherlessness and entered one of mothering. I gained a deeper understanding of my mother as a woman and through that, of myself.

Did my mother love me? To this fundamental question I respond unequivocally, "Yes." Did she love every single thing I did? No, of course she did not. But I give myself permission to have made mistakes in my life, to have erred and exercised poor judgment at times. That same permission, which is known as being human, I extend to my mother. She, like the rest of us, was fallible in her judgments at times and unable to love unconditionally.

Setting Our Children Free

As a mother, I know I must give my son that same permission—to try, to fail, to make mistakes, to experience regret. It is the challenge of parenting. We empower our children to the point that they do not need us any more. In order to love them best, we have to give them the thing that sometimes breaks our hearts: their freedom.

That becomes nearly impossible, I believe, unless we are healed at the core. Otherwise, there is too much temptation to cling when one should let go, to hold back when one should empower, to overprotect when one should set free.

We use the term "dysfunctional" to describe virtually every family. I sometimes wonder what a "functional" family is. But I do know that there is a tremendous need to heal our families at the heart, to have loving mothers and fathers under the same roof and children who feel cherished and protected. It is so easy to say and yet so hard to carry out.

In his book *Bradshaw On: The Family*, John Bradshaw talks about the need to explore without judgment the negative or dysfunctional behaviors that stretch from generation to generation. It exists in nearly every family, passed on like blue eyes and the heirloom silver. What would happen, I wonder, if we collectively decided to stop? What would happen if we put aside every negative behavior, hurtful criticism and abusive action? There would be nothing less than a fundamental shift in our society.

The Walking Wounded

I am certainly not the only one with this idea. Many other people from politicians to clergy, sociologists to talk-show hosts, have decried the break-up of the nuclear family. If it unravels, they say, there goes society. I have no doubt that they are right. While some look to the future for answers, I believe we must first deal with the past. There are too many wounded people walking around, blindly linking up with other wounded people to find love and stop the pain. If they stay together long enough to have children, the number of wounded people increases exponentially.

Healing can and will come from a variety of sources. The collective soul-searching that is going on in our culture, particularly as the baby boomers age and seek greater meaning in their lives, may very well lead to a spiritual renaissance in this society. For many of us, that renaissance (the word literally means rebirth) will send us back to the beginning: to our mothers. We experience a healing at our core and bring the nurturing back into our lives. We become spiritually, emotionally and psychologically replenished. Unhealthy ties to other people no longer satisfy us, and we cease to cultivate them. We extend to others in our family the honesty we experienced in dealing with our feelings about our mothers. We see our fathers and siblings from a new perspective, as adults on the path with us.

That is why I believe the Path of Understanding is not a journey we take just for ourselves. Consciously or not, we travel this road for each other, our friends, spouses, lovers and, most of all, for those who will come after us. One need not be a mother to be part of the generational links. In our behaviors and even our thoughts, we teach and influence those around us.

In her book A *Woman's Worth*, author and lecturer Marianne Williamson writes, "We don't have to give birth to children to know we're the mothers of the world. We are the wombs of the generations that follow, not only physically but emotionally, psychologically and spiritually. . . . The world is meant to be a safe and nurturing environment for children. The fact that it isn't is a sacred call to action for every conscious woman."

We begin with our own healing. At peace with ourselves, we act and live peacefully. Open to love in our lives, we bestow love on others. Our families are unified and healed. We will not be perfect parents; no such creature exists on this planet. But any mistakes we make will be from love, just as they often were for our mothers. The Path of Understanding has shown us the vast difference between a loving mistake, such as being overprotective, and a malicious one, such as deliberately cutting down a daughter's self-confidence to keep her subservient to her mother.

The Preciousness of Time

There is another lesson that is learned along the Path of Understanding, and that is the inestimable value of time.

Daughters whose mothers are deceased have tasted mortality. Our time on this earth is not unlimited. As an anonymous English monk wrote in the fourteenth century in the mystic classic *The Cloud of Unknowing,* "Nothing is more precious than time. In some small particle of time, little as it is, heaven can be won and lost. This is a sign that time is precious: God, who is the giver of time, never gives two particles of time together, but one after another."

It is an admonishment for us not to waste the time we have been given, however long or short it turns out to be. That is not, as I once believed, the crack of the whip over our heads to do more, see more, create more, accomplish more. Rather, it is a wake-up call to invest our time wisely. Sometimes that means work and other times it means play. I am grateful to my son for teaching me the value of play. There was still much more work that needed to be done this evening when I sat down in the living room to watch *Space Jam* for what seemed like the 110th time. Patrick wiggled and giggled and climbed all over me.

I do not want him to remember me only at the keyboard or running out the door to catch the early morning train to downtown Chicago. I choose to make time to reflect, relax and enjoy, which sometimes is harder for me to do than work. But it is a lesson that I have learned on the Path of Understanding. As I gained greater self-acceptance and self-love, I no longer gauged my worth by what I had accomplished. That is a measure that no one can live by, since we are never satisfied with what we have done.

Rather, my value to myself and to those around me is my ability to love and be loved. Love is not just a feeling; it is an action. It propels energy, healing and nurturing into the world. It extends between us, among us, through us and for us. It never wears out, and the supply can never be exhausted.

Each of our human relationships has the capacity to reflect the essence of God, the Source of all love. It is particularly true between mothers, the vessels of life, and their children. No matter how imperfect our mothers were or how flawed our relationship with them was, they were the source of our being-ness. They were the conduit through which our very selves flowed. Without them, we would not exist. In the same way, through us the next generation takes its place. Through our own spiritual, emotional and psychological healing, our legacy to the next generation is love.

Works Cited

Bradshaw, John. *Bradshaw On: The Family*. Deerfield Beach, Fla.: Health Communications, Inc., 1996.

Breathnach, Sarah Ban. *Simple Abundance: A Daybook of Comfort and Joy*. New York: Warner Books, Inc., 1995.

Choquette, Sonia. Interview conducted in June 1997.

Eadie, Betty. *Embraced by the Light*. New York: Bantam Books, 1994.

Estés, Clarissa Pinkola. *Women Who Run with the Wolves: Myths and Stories of the Wild Woman Archetype*. New York: Ballantine Books, 1992.

Friday, Nancy. *My Mother/My Self: The Daughter's Search for Identity*. New York: HarperCollins, 1977.

————. *The Power of Beauty*. New York: HarperCollins, 1996.

Friedan, Betty. *The Feminine Mystique: Twentieth Anniversary Edition*. New York: W. W. Norton & Company, 1983.

Goodwin, Doris Kearns. *No Ordinary Time — Franklin & Eleanor Roosevelt: The Home Front in World War II*. New York: Simon & Schuster, 1995.

Harvey, Brett. *The Fifties: A Women's Oral History*. New York: Harper-Collins, 1993.

Jung, C. G. *Aspects of the Feminine*. Princeton, N.J.: Princeton University Press, 1982.

Karr, Mary. *The Liars' Club: A Memoir*. New York: Penguin Books, 1995.

Kübler-Ross, Elisabeth. *On Death and Dying*. New York: Scribner, 1997.

———. *The Wheel of Life: A Memoir of Living and Dying*. New York: Bantam, 1998.

LaBelle, Patti. *Don't Block the Blessings: Revelations of a Lifetime*. New York: Boulevard Books, 1996.

Leach, Penelope. *Your Baby & Child: From Birth to Age Five*. New York: Knopf, 1997.

Maynard, Joyce. "Nobody's Daughter Anymore," *Domestic Affairs Newsletter* [*www.joycemaynard.com*].

Mueller, Lisel. "The Garden." In *Alive Together*. Baton Rouge, La.: Louisiana State University Press, 1996.

Peck, M. Scott. *The Road Less Traveled: A New Psychology of Love, Traditional Values and Spiritual Growth*. New York: Simon & Schuster, 1978.

Popcorn, Faith and Lys Marigold. *Clicking: 16 Trends to Future Fit Your Life, Your Work, and Your Business*. New York: HarperCollins, 1996.

Sischy, Ingrid. "Madonna and Child." *Vanity Fair*, March 1998.

Troy-Smith, Jean. *Called to Healing: Reflections on the Power of Earth's Stories in Women's Lives*. Oswego, N.Y.: State University of New York Press, 1996.

Van Praagh, James. *Talking to Heaven: A Medium's Message of Life After Death*. New York: Dutton, Penguin Group, 1997.

Walsh, James, ed. *The Cloud of Unknowing*. New York: Paulist Press, 1981.

Wells, Rebecca. *Divine Secrets of the Ya-Ya Sisterhood*. New York: Harper-Perennial, 1997.

Williamson, Marianne. *A Woman's Worth*. New York: Ballantine Books, 1993.

About the Author

*P*atricia Commins is a freelance business writer and a former correspondent for Reuters America Inc. During her career as a journalist, her articles appeared in *The New York Times*, *Boston Globe* and *Houston Chronicle*.

A journalist for twenty years, Ms. Commins began her career at the age of seventeen as a reporter at the *Palladium-Times*, a small daily newspaper in northern New York State. With a liberal arts degree from the State University of New York, she continued her journalistic career in New York City and, more recently, Chicago.

Her essays on Africa, Berlin and Switzerland have been published in the *Christian Science Monitor*. Feature stories on rock star Jim Morrison's grave and cross-country skiing have appeared on the Leisure & Arts Page of *The Wall Street Journal*.

Remembering Mother, Finding Myself: A Journey of Love and Self-Acceptance, which was inspired by her journey to reconnect with her mother who died when the author was twenty-six, reflects Ms. Commins' desire to write books that teach, heal and inspire. Ms. Commins has finished *Memorial Day*, a psychological suspense novel about a clairvoyant woman who tries to free herself from the past that entraps her.

Ms. Commins lives in suburban Chicago with her husband, Kevin, and son, Patrick.

Ms. Commins welcomes your stories about your mother and yourself. Contact her via e-mail at: *Remember©sprynet.com* or at P.O. Box 414, Park Ridge, IL 60068.